THE OAKWOOD PRESS

HARROW & WEALDSTONE 50 YEARS ON

Clearing up the Aftermath

by
Peter Tatlow

In memory of those tragically killed in this accident; also dedicated to those who lost loved ones and who suffered injury as a consequence; and in honour of those who calmly released and cared for the casualties and those who manfully struggled to restore the line.

THE OAKWOOD PRESS

© Oakwood Press & Peter Tatlow 2008

First Edition 2002
Second Edition 2008

British Library Cataloguing in Publication Data
A Record for this book is available from the British Library
ISBN 978 0 85361 680 1

Typeset by Oakwood Graphics.
Repro by Ford Graphics, Ringwood, Hants.
Printed by Cambrian Printers, Aberystwyth, Ceredigion.

All rights reserved. No part of this book may be reproduced or transmitted in any form or by any means, electronic or mechanical, including photocopying, recording or by any information storage and retrieval system, without permission from the Publisher in writing.

Note on the Author

Peter Tatlow is well known for his contribution to railway research over 45 years. An interest in railways and railway modelling has been his main pastime since he can remember. Some of his earliest memories are of journeys undertaken during World War II. Following military service in the Royal Engineers, he joined the Chief Civil Engineer's Department of the Southern Region of British Railways. He left BR over 10 years later having qualified as a chartered civil engineer and then worked on the design and construction of bridges, both in United Kingdom and overseas. He is now retired from full-time employment.

With the decline of the steam locomotive on BR, his thoughts turned back to the inter-war period and his attention has been directed to some of the other facets of the railway scene. Although his stated preference is for the LMS (Highland Section) between the wars, finding a gap in the published information on LNER wagons he has with the assistance of other members of the LNER Study Group redressed the balance, initially by a series of articles in the model press and subsequently with the publication in 1976 of his first book *LNER Wagons*.

Since then he has had published numerous articles in the prototype and model railway press and specialist journals on a wide range of subjects including locomotives, coaches, wagons, travelling cranes, bridges, train ferries and civil engineering activities. He has seven further books to his name: *A History of Highland Locomotives*, OPC 1979; *Highland Railway Miscellany*, OPC 1985; compiled *Historic Carriage Drawings, Volume 3 – Non-Passenger Coaching Stock*, Pendragon 2000; *Harrow & Wealdstone Accident, 50 years on, Clearing up the aftermath*, The Oakwood Press, 2002; *St John's Lewisham, 50 years on, Restoring traffic*, The Oakwood Press, 2007; and is currently revisiting his first work with *An Illustrated History of LNER Wagons* in four volumes, the first two of which were published by Wild Swan in 2005 and 2007.

Front Cover: On 8th October, 1952 a double collision between a local and two express trains occurred at Harrow & Wealdstone station, leading to the second worst railway accident in Great Britain. The mangled wreckage produced called for the efforts of four railway steam breakdown cranes to handle the larger items of wreckage in the clearing up operation. The 36 ton crane from Kentish Town and 50 ton crane from Willesden are hooked up to No. 46202 *Princess Anne*, while on the right behind the coach Crewe North's 50 ton breakdown crane clears the fast lines. *London Midland Region, BR*
Rear cover: When the Sanctuary of Christchurch in North Watford was remodelled in 1953, the work was carried out as a memorial to the 112 people who lost their lives in the accident. As well as a plaque elsewhere in the church, this pane in the East stained glass window was altered to record that it was a memorial. *Courtesy the Vicar of Christchurch, Watford*

Published by The Oakwood Press (Usk), P.O. Box 13, Usk, Mon., NP15 1YS.
E-mail: sales@oakwoodpress.co.uk
Website: www.oakwoodpress.co.uk

Contents

	Foreword to First Edition *by Alan Earnshaw*	4
	Preface	5
	Introduction	7
Chapter One	Harrow & Wealdstone Station and Signalling	9
Chapter Two	The Locomotives and Rolling Stock	15
	The Post-War Scene	17
Chapter Three	The Accident	21
	The Double Collision	21
	Initial Reaction of Railway Staff	30
Chapter Four	The Response	33
	Press Activities	33
	Mounting the Rescue Operation	34
	Medical Assistance	35
	The American Air Force Contribution	37
	Casualties and their Removal	39
	Ambulance Work	46
	Police Activities	47
	Casualty Enquiry Offices	50
	Assistance by Others and Visitors	51
Chapter Five	Personal Recollections	55
Chapter Six	Clearing the Wreckage	63
	Disruption and Traffic Diversions	83
	Spiritual and Psychological Aspects	89
	Subsequent Clearing Up Operations	93
	Sole Surviving Locomotive	101
Chapter Seven	Official Responses	103
	Coroner's Court	103
	The Ministry of Transport Inspector's Investigation	103
Chapter Eight	Automatic Warning System	110
Chapter Nine	Conclusions	114
	Postscript	117
Appendix One	Composition of the Trains	120
Appendix Two	Train Diversions	122
Appendix Three	The Railway Executive's Response to the Inquiry Recommendations	124
Appendix Four	A Letter from Signalman Armitage	125
	Acknowledgements	126
	Bibliography	126
	Index	127

Foreword to First Edition

This summer of 2002 will be remembered for street parties and celebrations for the 50th Anniversary of Queen Elizabeth II, who came to the throne after the tragic early death of her father HM King George VI on 6th February, 1952. However, for transport historians 1952 is a marked year, for on 8th October a multiple train collision occurred at Harrow & Wealdstone station. This incident came to be recorded as the worst-ever railway disaster on English soil, as 112 passengers and railwaymen were killed and over 200 were injured.

It was the culmination to a disastrous year that started badly when a twelve-day vigil by the captain of *The Flying Enterprise* ended on 10th January when his ship sank off Falmouth as it was being towed towards safety by a rescue tug, but the national headlines were then dominated by a court case involving a fatal coach accident. After crashing his vehicle into a troop of Marine Cadets at Chatham, Kent - killing 23 of them - the driver was fined just £20 and banned from driving for three years on 22nd January. In May BOAC introduced passenger jet travel with the new de Havilland Comet, but this was to be followed by a series of tragic crashes as the aircraft was dogged by problems. Disaster returned in the summer, and 31 people died after a cloudburst over Exmoor resulted in a freak flood sweeping down the Lyn valley in North Devon, devastating the town of Lynmouth on 16th August. Six weeks later, on 29th September, John Cobb the 52-year-old speed ace died whilst taking his jet-powered boat *Crusader* down Loch Ness at 240 mph during a world water speed record attempt. In the air industry de Havilland experienced further problems, this time with their 110 Jet Fighter, when one that was being displayed at the Farnborough Air Show blew up as it broke the sound barrier. Wreckage showered down on the 150,000 strong crowd, killing 26 of them in addition to the two pilots. During the winter months an unseen killer was bad air pollution, manifested by the London Smog, which resulted in 1,268 hospital deaths alone in the inner London area during 1952.

Disasters such as these repulse and fascinate people! Some are filled with morbid curiosity, others have a desire to study history and see what lessons can be learned from it. As the author of five books on railway accidents and disaster, I soon came to the conclusion that important lessons are to be learned from the detailed study of disastrous events, for in reality there is no such thing as a new accident. Most accidents have some historical precedent, and more importantly most have a means of prevention if only the lessons of the past are carefully studied and applied. It is therefore welcoming to read works like Peter Tatlow's new account of the Harrow & Wealdstone Disaster, as it provides yet another vital warning from the past. Thankfully many of the causes that can be attributed to the events leading up to that fateful day 50 years ago can no longer be repeated! Valuable lessons were learned and new procedures put in place, but we can never ever afford to be complacent when considering the safety of the travelling public. Peter has obviously taken this view in his careful, analytical study of the accident and its aftermath, and he has not sensationalised the account in any way. Therefore his sensitive and respectful record can easily be recommended to the general public, but to railway enthusiasts, regular train passengers and railway professionals it really should be considered as obligatory reading.

Professor Alan Earnshaw, PhD, MSc, Grad.ISM

Preface

It is now more than 50 years since the appalling accident at Harrow & Wealdstone on 8th October, 1952. Enough has probably already been written about the causes of it and the steps taken following the accident to avoid recurrence, so instead this book will look at the huge task of mounting the rescue operation, managing the disruption to railway operations and clearing up the aftermath.

During World War II, with the beaches barricaded and mined against German invasion, seaside holidays were of limited value. I came to know the West Coast main line, however, when evacuated to the Isle of Bute in September 1940 for 18 months; later during the war when my mother took my brother and me on several short breaks to stay with our maternal grandparents at Bushey in Hertfordshire; immediately following the cessation of hostilities overnight journeys to and from Oban for a fortnight's holiday on the Isle of Mull; and in July 1952 to Penrith for a scout camp beside Ullswater. At Bushey my grandmother was residing at Grove End, a residential guest house, in Bushey Hall Road, to escape the bombing of London. To two small boys considerable interest was aroused by, and time spent watching, the comings and goings through the gate house to a United States Army Air Force base directly across the road. At weekends my father would join us from London and I have special memories of being taken on Saturday mornings to the well-known bridge overlooking the water troughs at Bushey on the West Coast main line from Euston of the former London & North Western Railway (LNWR), by then part of the London Midland and Scottish Railway (LMS). Here a procession of steam-hauled express and local passenger and freight trains could be observed on the up and down fast and slow lines, whilst LMS electric suburban and London Transport tube stock scuttled by on the electric lines.

Harrow & Wealdstone station following the reconstruction carried out during 1911/12 to provide additional tracks for the Electric lines. The work may not yet be complete, as the tracks in the foreground do not have conductor rails. The passengers standing on the platform, 50 years later, would have been waiting to board the local train from Tring to Euston. The impact between the overnight train from Perth and the local train occurred to the left of the station nameboard. *Brian Girling Collection*

By 1952 I was travelling daily by Southern electric trains to school in Leatherhead and, on seeing the headlines of the railway disaster at Harrow & Wealdstone station on 8th October, purchased my own copy of the *Daily Telegraph* the next day. A growing interest in railways as a whole, Hornby-Dublo model trains and the writings of the Reverend Edward Beal in particular, had already made me aware of the work of steam breakdown cranes and here in the newspapers were vivid pictures of these machines, fulfilling their calling, by removing wreckage to enable the injured to be released, the dead removed and in due course helping to clear and restore the line.

Later military service in the Royal Engineers ensued with a posting under American Air Force officers at the headquarters of Allied Forces Central Europe at Fontainebleau, France. Subsequently I joined the Chief Civil Engineer's Department of the Southern Region of British Railways. Despite the collapse of the flyover within two months at St John's, Lewisham following the impact of a locomotive tender derailed as a result of a collision, I was fortunately never personally involved in an event as catastrophic as Harrow & Wealdstone, but did become familiar with the use of breakdown cranes for bridge works and re-railing errant vehicles.

The enormity of the task facing the railway, emergency services and local community in dealing with the immediate effects of the accident at Harrow has never ceased to amaze me. The more I have researched the event in preparation for this book, the more one has come to recognise the magnificent way in which they responded. Whilst in no way wishing to take away from the tragedy of loss of life and the suffering of the bereaved and injured, let us pay tribute to those who tackled the task of clearing up the physical and emotional chaos created by the second most serious railway accident in the British Isles.

It was pleasing in 2004 to have the first edition of this book short-listed, to one of three, for the Railway & Canal Historical Society's first annual Transport History Book of the Year Award, sponsored by the David St John Thomas Charitable Trust. This encouraged me to consider another work in the same vein and The Oakwood Press were kind enough in 2007 to publish *St John's Lewisham, 50 years on, Restoring traffic* (ISBN 978 0 85361 669 6), likewise to commemorate its 50th anniversary of that equally sad event. In turn this has aroused interest in my earlier work and led to an invitation to revise and reprint this book.

During the intervening five years, numerous readers have kindly contacted me with their thoughts, comments and recollections of this tragic event and I have included some, where appropriate, in this new edition, together with additional material that has also come to light since publication of the first edition.

Peter Tatlow
March 2008

Introduction

Fifty years ago the second most serious accident in the history of the railways of Britain, and worst in peacetime, occurred on the West Coast main line at Harrow & Wealdstone station, 11¼ miles from the London terminus of Euston, in which 112 lives were lost. This figure has only once been exceeded, when another double collision took place at Quintinshill, also on the West Coast main line north of Carlisle, in 1915 during World War I. On that occasion 227 people were killed and fire among gas-lit wooden coaches, many filled with troops destined for the Dardanelles and the horrors of the landings at Gallipoli, was a major factor in adding to the loss of life. At Harrow, for reasons still not adequately explained, the driver of an overnight sleeper train from Perth to London, in conditions of patchy fog overran signals and collided at speed into the rear of a crowded stationary outer suburban train. This had no sooner happened, than the double-headed express train to Liverpool and Manchester, gathering speed on its way out of Euston, ran into the wreckage obstructing the adjacent line.

For younger readers it may be difficult to visualise foggy conditions during the autumn and winter months in the days before the Clean Air Act of 1956. Prior to the general adoption of gas or oil fired central heating, open coal fires were almost universal in homes around the country and much of industry still depended on coal-fired furnaces to produce its own power on site, all of which contributed to pollution of the atmosphere and, in certain weather conditions, severe choking fog. Indeed, dreadful as this accident was, it pales into insignificance when compared with the 4,000 people in London overall it has been alleged died in hospital and at home as a result of such conditions over a period of only two weeks in December 1952, and now generally recognised as a conservative estimate, just two months after the accident. On the day of the accident, fog was widespread through the night and early morning in the Midlands and the northern Home Counties. At the time of the collisions it had been clearing fairly quickly at Harrow as the sun burnt it off. It is reported that the visibility around the station varied from about 200 yards to 300 yards or more, though it was probably more restricted in the open country in the vicinity of the up distant signals. The wind that morning was slight and therefore did not assist in the dispersal of the fog.

Considerable public outcry ensued following the accident and this undoubtedly hastened the introduction of the automatic warning system, which was anyway already in an advanced stage of development. It is not the main purpose of this work to rake over the cause and effect of this accident yet again, but rather to take a closer look at the immediate consequences of the event and how the railway and emergency services coped with rescuing the wounded and clearing the wreckage to enable the line to be reopened to traffic. First, however, let us look at the plant and infrastructure involved in the accident.

In LNWR days, the signalman reaches out to a Fletcher's three position block instrument in Harrow No. 1 signal box. The same instruments were still in use when the accident occurred. The diagram above them, however, only shows a pair of single crossovers from up slow to down slow and on to the up fast, instead of the double crossover from the up slow to up fast and down fast to down slow lines.

LNWR Society

Chapter One

Harrow & Wealdstone Station and Signalling

Except for a short distance at the outset, there were generally six tracks over the 17½ miles between Euston and Watford Jn signalled for the running of passenger trains. From Willesden, 5⅜ miles from Euston, their order on the formation is from east to west: up slow, down slow, up fast and down fast, whilst the up electric and down electric start from there on the east side, but pass under the others between Stonebridge Park and Wembley so that by Harrow & Wealdstone they are on the west side of the fast lines and continue northward on the same formation as far as Bushey, 16 miles from Euston. Here the electric lines diverge to the west, rejoining the main route as they approach Watford Junction station, where the electric lines terminate. From Watford the four tracks continue northward through Tring and on to Roade Junction, 32 miles and 60 miles from Euston respectively.

Harrow was one of the original stations on the London and Birmingham Railway opened between Euston and Boxmoor on 20th July, 1837. Four years later six trains per weekday and two on Sundays in each direction called at the station. Built as double track, increases in traffic led first to the construction of a down goods line from Primrose Hill to Watford in 1858, followed by quadruple track by 1875 to cater for its growing long distance passenger and freight business. It became the junction in the trailing direction for the branch line to Stanmore on 18th December, 1890, but the LNWR generally displayed no great interest in providing for the traffic of workers from the Metropolis who wished to reside in the ever expanding suburbs, or as we should know them now – commuters, being instead fully occupied handling the prodigious freight traffic on offer. For instance, it was only under LMS management that stations were opened at Belmont, on the Stanmore branch, on 15th September, 1932; South Kenton on 3rd July, 1933; and Apsley north of Watford on 26th September, 1938.

It took the threatened encroachment of an electric tube railway, with an extension from Golder's Green to Watford, to buck up its ideas. This led to the construction of the electrified lines from Broad Street and Euston to Watford Jn, which were shared with the London Electric Railway, today known as the Bakerloo Line of London Underground. At Harrow these 'new' lines were laid on the west side of the main line. To accommodate them, due to a lack of space, the four existing main lines had to be slewed to the east to enable the new lines to occupy the formation of the old fast lines. A further line on the east side was provided for the terminating Stanmore branch trains, together with two sidings between the electric lines to the north of the station upon which to stable electric trains.

This necessitated the reconstruction of the station from 1910 to 1912 in the form that it was at the time of the accident and, apart from the lifting of the Stanmore branch, largely still is today. By now it consisted of one single-sided platform with the original station buildings of 1837 on the west side and three island platforms with the usual facilities, together with more station buildings and clock tower, on the east side. The goods yard was at the country end also on the east side. Bridge No. 42, a multi-span bridge carried Wealdstone High Street across the line at the

Harrow No. 1 signal box as seen from the down fast line adjacent to the point where at 8.18 am on 8th October, 1952 the late running overnight express from Perth, having overrun adverse signals, collided with the rear of the local suburban train from Tring to Euston. *M.S. Welch*

The end of platform 1 with Harrow No. 2 signal box on the left opposite the turnouts from electric lines leading to a double slip and berthing sidings at country end of station in 1950. The two locomotives of the Liverpool and Manchester express careered across the platform on the right and destroyed the double slip. *J.E. Cull, courtesy HMRS*

platform ends towards Euston, while the two station buildings were connected to the platforms by footbridge No. 43. At about the turn of the century before last, the name was extended to Harrow & Wealdstone, perhaps to distinguish it from Harrow on the Hill opened by the Metropolitan Railway in 1880. The signal box Harrow No. 1 for the main line was situated at the country end of platform Nos. 4 and 5 between the up fast and down slow lines, whilst affairs on the electric lines were controlled by Harrow No. 2 on the down (west) side. Electric trains from Broad Street and the tube to Watford Junction ran from 16th April, 1917, but it was not until 10th July, 1922 that LNWR electric trains departed from Euston.

Previous incidents at Harrow have included a collision in 1840 when, during single line working, a double-headed goods train for London running 'wrong-line' collided head on with the engine of a stationary train in the station facing in the opposite direction, resulting in the death of two railwaymen. A boiler to long boiler 0-6-0 locomotive No. 878, built in 1853, exploded in the station itself on 5th May, 1862. A further collision occurred on 26th November, 1870 when six people were killed.

In 1952 manual block working was still in use on the main lines with semaphore stop signals and, for the most part, colour light distant signals. The electric lines were generally automatically signalled with colour lights and continuous track circuiting with Harrow No. 2 signal box to control entry into the berthing sidings.

In Harrow No. 1 signal box the four block instruments were of the three-position needle type, each of the four bells of different tone, rung respectively from Hatch End and North Wembley for up and down trains and for both the fast and slow lines. By the time of the accident, the standard Class C interlocked block controls of the former London Midland and Scottish Railway had been installed in practically all the mechanical signal boxes on the West Coast route. The purpose of their design was to prevent a train from entering an occupied section, as the result of a signalman's mistake. This was achieved by only allowing one operation for the acceptance of a train by the signalman at the far end of the section; only allowing such acceptance if either the first stop signal worked from the box concerned was already at danger, or the lever working it was in the normal position (at Harrow on the up fast line the acceptance of a train from Hatch End proved the lever of the up fast outer home was normal *and* its arm was properly at danger); and interlocking between successive stop signals worked from the same box to ensure that none can be cleared for a train unless that next ahead of it had been returned to danger.

Track circuits ensured that the 'Train on Line' indication was displayed on the block instrument while the section of track on the approach to the home signal was occupied. Likewise, with the outer home signal at danger, it sounded a buzzer in the signal box and also maintained that indication after departure of the train, until action was taken by the signalman to alter it.

The signal lever frame in the signal box included mechanical interlocking designed to prevent conflicting movements. For instance, the setting up of the road to allow a train to cross from the up slow to the up fast could not be achieved if the signals on the up fast in the rear, i.e. further back, together with those on the down slow, were not already at danger and would subsequently have prevented the signalman from moving them until the train had moved forward and was protected by further signals in advance, i.e. further forward.

Newly-constructed Stanier 2-8-0 locomotive No. 8004 hauls a through freight past Harrow & Wealdstone station on the up fast line sometime before World War II. The rear of the train is still coming through the same cross-over that the ill-fated local passenger train was to take on 8th October, 1952, while the engine has about reached the spot where the Perth train collided with it. As seen here the engine, with dome-less vertical throat-plate boiler, has yet to be fitted with vacuum brake and is presumably still classed '7F', later reclassified '8F'. An ex-LNWR electric train is stabled in the berthing sidings to the left. *Author's Collection*

No. 40043 ex-LMS Fowler '3MT' 2-6-2T waits with a motor train on a sunny day for passengers at Stanmore in 1952, shortly before the passenger service was curtailed to Belmont, the last train through to Stanmore running on 13th September, three weeks before the accident. A train from Belmont on the morning of 8th October that year arrived at Harrow & Wealdstone station moments after the accident. *J.A.G.H. Coltas*

HARROW & WEALDSTONE STATION AND SIGNALLING

The levers in Harrow No. 1 signal frame, which faced towards the fast lines, are given below, their location being shown in Figure 1 (*page 62*):

Lever No.	Colour	Description Signal	Type of from box	Direction
-	-	Fixed Distant	semaphore	South
A	Red	Stanmore branch to goods yard	shunt signal	South
-	-	Fixed Home	semaphore	South
B	Blue	Stanmore branch catch points	-	South
C	Red	Goods yard to Stanmore branch	shunt signal	North
1	Yellow	Down Fast Distant	colour light	South
2	Red	Down Fast Outer Home	semaphore	South
3	Red	Down Fast Inner Home	semaphore	South
4	Red	Down Fast Starter	semaphore	North
5	White	Spare	-	-
6	Red	Down Fast to Down Slow Inner Home	semaphore	South
7	Yellow	Down Slow Distant	colour light	South
8	Red	Down Slow Outer Home	semaphore	South
9	Red	Down Slow Inner Home	semaphore	South
10	Red	Down Slow Starter	semaphore	North
11	Black & White	Down Fast detonator placer	-	Outside box
12	Black & White	Down Slow detonator placer	-	Outside box
13	Black & White	Up Slow detonator placer	-	Outside box
14	White	Spare	-	-
15	Blue	16 Points Unlocked - Locked	-	North
16	Black	Down Fast to Down Slow	-	North
17	Black	Down Slow from Down Fast	-	North
18	Black	Up Fast from Up Slow	-	North
19	Black	Up Slow to Up Fast	-	North
20	Blue	19 Points Unlocked - Locked	-	North
21	Red	Down Slow or goods yard	dwarf signal	South
22	Black	Slow lines trailing crossing	-	North
23	Black	Up Slow & Shunting Neck crossing	-	North
24	Red	Shunting Neck to Up Slow	disc signal	North
25	White	Spare (formerly shunt through)	(shunt signal)	(North)
26	Red	Shunting Neck to Down Slow	disc signal	North
27	Black	Shunting Neck Crossing	-	North
28	Black	Down Slow Crossing	-	North
29	Red	Set Back Down Slow to Sidings	disc signal	North
30	Red	Set Back Up Slow to Sidings	disc signal	North
31	Black	Up Slow Crossing	-	North
32	Black	Shunting Neck Crossing	-	North
33	Red	Shunting Neck to Up Slow	disc signal	North
34	Red	Up Slow Advanced Starter	semaphore	South
35	Red	Up Slow Starter	semaphore	South
36	Red	Up Slow Home	semaphore	North
37	Yellow	Up Slow Distant	colour light	North
38	Red	Up Slow to Up Fast Home	semaphore	North
39	White	Spare	-	-
40	Black & White	Up Fast detonator placer	-	Outside box
41	Red	Up Fast Advanced Starter	semaphore	South
42	Red	Up Fast Starter	semaphore	South
43	Red	Up Fast Inner Home	semaphore	North
44	Red	Up Fast Outer Home	semaphore	North
45	Yellow	Up Fast Distant	colour light	North

Notes: Levers A, B and C released by key on staff for the Stanmore branch.
The colour of the signal lever indicates their purpose as follows: red - stop signal, shunting signal; yellow distant signal; black - points; blue - facing point lock, clearance bar, gate stop and wickets or catch points; black with white chevrons (pointing upwards for the up lines and downwards for the down lines) - detonator placers; white - spare.

An extract from a pre-Grouping edition of the Railway Clearing House map of Britain which shows lines to the north and west of London. Harrow & Wealdstone can be found to the south of Watford on the LNWR main line. (See also *Figure 7* on page 90.)

To improve the visibility of distant signals on high speed main lines, colour light distant signals had, with few exceptions, been provided throughout the length of the West Coast main line between London and Carlisle in fulfilment of a programme initiated by the London Midland and Scottish Railway before World War II. Apart from their intrinsic brilliance, colour light signals have the advantage that they can be positioned and aligned closer to the driver's eye and line of sight. They are therefore much more conspicuous than oil-lit semaphores, particularly at night and in fog. As a result the usual fog handsignalling arrangements at distant signals were not considered necessary where colour light distant signals had been installed.

The beam from the main aspect of a colour light was designed to focus to a limited spread of 4 degrees, resulting in a narrow cone of light, as anything wider would lead to an unacceptable loss of light intensity. As the driver drew close to the signal, he would lose the full effect of the main beam. So to compensate for this, a 'hot strip' of special prisms in a limited quadrant was incorporated into the main signal lens to direct a separate intense wedge-shaped beam of light towards him as he passed. Where the approach to a colour light signal is on a curve, the alignment of a such narrow beam is a matter of compromise. Generally the beam was aligned horizontally so that its central axis lies across the near side rail on the approach side (50 yards) of the signal close by, resulting in the edge of the beam crossing the near side rail some considerable distance from the signal.

At Harrow all four of the distant signals were colour light and were carried on gantries spanning the two lines to which the signals referred. In the up direction, the up fast (No. 45) and up slow (No. 37) were located on a gantry 1,474 yards from the up fast outer home (No. 44), which was a sufficient distance to enable a train travelling at 75 mph to brake and come to a stand on the falling gradient of 1 in 339. So a driver approaching Harrow would first see the main beam at a range of 600 yards, after which the intensity of the light would steadily increase until he was 50 yards from the signal.

Chapter Two

The Locomotives and Rolling Stock

Two of the early classes of locomotive introduced by William A. Stanier, following his appointment as Chief Mechanical Engineer of the LMS on 1st January, 1932, were the 4-6-2 '7P' 'Princess Royal' Pacifics and 4-6-0 '5XPs', subsequently to be known as 'Jubilees', each being reclassified '8P' and '6P' respectively by British Railways in 1951. The 'Princess Royals' were the first of Stanier's designs to be produced and were intended to be an advance on the 'Royal Scot' class of 4-6-0 as the top flight machines on the fastest and most prestigious passenger trains. The third example of the class was completed in June 1935 as an experimental steam turbine locomotive and ran successfully for many years, often on the Euston-Liverpool expresses. By the time of the accident, however, it had just been rebuilt as a conventional reciprocating engine more or less like its sisters. Stanier's third design was a development of the three-cylinder parallel-boilered 'Patriot' class used on express trains in support of the 'Royal Scots' and had entered traffic in May 1934. No. 5637 *Windward Islands*, as one of the eventual 191 members of the 'Jubilee' class, was built in December that year.

No more turbine-powered locomotives were supplied to the LMS, but, after the building of 10 more of the reciprocating version, the design was developed into the streamlined super Pacific required to haul the 'Coronation Scot' high speed train between London and Glasgow put into service during the summer of 1937. Further members of this class were built in both streamlined and un-streamlined form until by 1948 there was a total of thirty-eight. During the more austere conditions prevailing following the war, however, the streamlined version was defrocked in the cause of ease of maintenance. No. 6242 *City of Glasgow* was initially a streamlined engine in crimson lake livery out-shopped from Crewe in May 1940. In March 1947 she had the streamlining removed and appeared in LMS lined black livery. At the time of the accident she was in the short-lived BR blue.

The last class involved in the disaster about to be considered, the class '4' parallel-boilered 2-6-4 passenger tank, predated Stanier and was considered to be one of the best of Sir Henry Fowler's designs, due in part at least to the inclusion of long travel valve gear. Indeed, the tapered boiler on Stanier's version is sometimes considered to be an inferior steam raiser. Both types were intended for short haul passenger work, such as outer suburban trains.

These four classes of locomotive were then among the leading types employed by the LMS prior to and during World War II.

During the LMS period main line corridor and local suburban bogie carriage stock, for the most part, consisted of wooden bodies mounted on steel underframes. Whilst developments, particularly in appearance, were made by the replacement of wood panelling by flush steel sheeting, the basic body structure still consisted of wooden framing on a separate steel underframe. British Railways on the other hand adopted all-steel welded bodies for its

An official view of LMS experimental non-condensing steam turbine locomotive No. 6202, which entered traffic in June 1935, as fitted with a domed boiler from July 1936 and prior to the fitting of smoke deflector plates in 1939. *London Midland Region, BR*

LMS No. 5637 *Windward Islands* in happier days, then shedded at Edge Hill, passes Ashton signal box, an intermediate block post on the West Coast main line south of Roade, with a down express excursion train No. W695 on 26th June, 1948. Perhaps, in view of the locomotive's allocation, the train was from Euston to Liverpool. *L. Hanson*

Mark I coaches, but still on a separate steel underframe, and these were just beginning to enter service at the time of the accident. However, as we shall see in the case of the Liverpool/Manchester train, rather than introducing the replacement of a complete train, individual vehicles seem to have been inserted into existing train sets, as the occasion demanded and availability permitted.

The Post-War Scene

The probability of war with Germany was becoming increasingly obvious by 1938 and the Government motivated the main line railway companies to consider the implications and, under the provisions of the Air Raid Precautions Act of that year, provided funding to enable preparations to be put in hand. During the conflict itself the railway companies' organisation and facilities, (together with those of the public emergency services), to clear up after the consequences of aerial bombardment were fully tested and experienced with dealing with such incidents. The public at large too had to some extent become inured to the sight of devastation and the consequent casualties.

During the war, particularly following the introduction of conscription, as would be expected the numbers of men and women serving in the armed forces rose to a high figure. On the cessation of hostilities in Europe and the Far East there was naturally a desire to return to civilian life and for a short while conscription was suspended. With the increase in tension between East and West, however, national service was reintroduced, so the sight of soldiers, sailors and airmen travelling about the country in uniform, often by train, was common. In 1952, with the forces of the United Nations pitted against the Communists in Korea, almost one million persons were in the British Army, Royal Navy and Royal Air Force, compared with a fifth of that figure today who no longer travel in uniform.

Mechanical dial telephone exchange systems had been introduced in a few areas of the country, particularly in London, prior to the war by the General Post Office (GPO) – forerunners of British Telecom. Whilst this enabled subscribers to dial automatic calls locally within the exchange area, any long distance call still had to be placed through operators in manually-operated exchanges. The railway also had its own telephone system, but at this period was even more archaic, many outlets being connected to an omnibus line with up to 16 outlets, where each had its own particular call sign. The development of mobile phones, that we are all so familiar with today, was a long way in the future. Radio receivers, or wirelesses as they were then known, were normally kept in the home and anyway could not be used to transmit. During the World War II 'walkie talkies' had been developed for short distance communication on the field of battle, but required a heavy pack on the operator's back. Longer distance radio communication, if not at a fixed location, still required equipment mounted in a motor vehicle.

Other arrangements set up under the provisions of the Air Raid Precautions Act of 1938 included the organisation of Civil Defence teams; the Auxiliary Fire Service; Women's Volunteer Service; and Fire Wardens. These had all done

LMS No. 6202 as most of us like to remember her when an unnamed steam turbine-powered locomotive seen here on 28th May, 1947 leaving Euston with the 8.30 am to Liverpool. By this time the casing to the reverse turbines, on the side shown, had been extended, to accommodate control equipment, and a pair of smoke deflectors had been fitted to lift drifting exhaust above the driver's line of sight. *Ken Nunn, courtesy LCGB*

The rebuilt Turbomotive No. 46202 re-entered service on 28th August, 1952 and at that time was given the name *Princess Anne*. This picture is presumed to have been taken at Shrewsbury during a running-in turn. The stepped running plate and quasi-'Duchess' class cover to the steam pipes should be noted. The latter appears not to have as clean lines as the originals. Perhaps the rather flatter surfaces envisaged the fitting of smoke deflector plates, but if so none were ever carried. *Courtesy Museum of Science and Industry, Birmingham*

sterling work during the war in coping with the consequences of the Blitz of 1940, subsequent intermittent bombing raids, flying-bombs of 1944 and V2 rockets. These arrangements remained in being in the post-war era in response to the threat of nuclear attack from the Soviet Block.

As an experimental locomotive, the turbine machinery of No. 6202, or 46202 as it had now become, had always been expensive to maintain and utilisation was much reduced, particularly during the war, while waiting for one-off replacement parts. By the spring of 1950 the turbines themselves had reached the end of their useful lives and, rather than install new ones, it was decided, having run 458,772 miles, to rebuild the engine with four-cylinder simple expansion reciprocating machinery, much as her half-sisters, but with some features of the later 'Coronation' class. Interestingly enough in its rebuilt form this engine had new frames giving the same axle spacing and cylinders of the class's successors, now termed 'Duchesses', but still retaining 6 ft 6 in. diameter wheels rather than 6 ft 9 in. of the latter. It was hence briefly, as we shall see, theoretically the most powerful engine in the country with a tractive effort at 85 per cent boiler pressure of 41,538 lb., eclipsing Gresley's ex-LNER 4-6-2-2 'W' class No. 60700 by just 101 lb., for all the difference this will have made in practical terms! In this form No. 46202 emerged from Crewe works in August 1952 and was named *Princess Anne*. On 28th August, 1952 it had been noted on its usual 8.30 am Euston-Liverpool train.

In September No. 46202 was photographed passing the shed at Tamworth with a Euston to Liverpool express train. A few weeks later, it was wrecked in the double collision at Harrow & Wealdstone, as result of which it was damaged beyond economic repair and withdrawn. *J.A.G.H. Coltas*

One of the photographs taken from the air looking down from the south-west on the accident, with hoards of rescuers working away to extract the dead and injured trapped in the wreckage. Fire engines and ambulances can be seen at both station entrances, while large numbers of members of the public, restrained by the Police, look on from a distance. The damage to the footbridge can be seen on the right.

Metropolitan Police Museum

Chapter Three

The Accident

The Double Collision

Robert S. Jones had started work on the LMS Railway in 1927 as an engine cleaner. He was passed for firing duties in 1934, but, as normal at those times, was not actually appointed fireman until three years later. After achieving 84 out of a possible 90 marks in his verbal and practical examination, when the minimum needed was only 65, he was passed to drive in August 1946, although again not formally taking up such a position until January 1948.

Once having been passed as a driver, Jones made it his job to become familiar with a wide range of the routes radiating from Crewe, including the West Coast main line to London Euston, which he had signed for on 31st March, 1950. In the next 2½ years he had made 41 trips along the line. Consistent with the work of Crewe North shed, these included 29 in charge of express passenger trains, 11 with parcels, empty stock or fast automatic brake fitted freight trains and just one light engine movement, most of which would, therefore, have used the fast lines, rather than the slow ones. By the autumn of 1952 he was at Crewe North shed in a spare link, from which drivers, subject to their having the route knowledge and having accordingly signed the route card, could be drawn upon at short notice to work special trains arranged by Control, or to fill the place of men otherwise absent on annual or sick leave. Rather than having a rostered booking on time based on the need to take an engine out for a specific turn, men in the spare link were allocated block times during which they might expect to be allocated a duty as the need arose.

As a young man he had been methodical showing a keen interest in his work and in his spare time regularly attended at mutual improvement classes. Outside working hours his main interest was his family and house. Of excellent health, his only sick leave over recent years appears to have been a bout of bronchitis in 1947. From this it can be seen that Jones was regarded as a steady, even-tempered reliable man, whose work as a driver was entirely satisfactory.

Following the whole weekend of 4th/5th October, 1952 off duty, early on the Monday driver Jones had worked a trip on the Liverpool line and booked off duty at 11.40 am. He was back on duty on early turn the Tuesday, to take the 4.25 am to Morecambe and had finished this duty at 2.40 pm, probably amounting to about 11 hours. Arriving home by bicycle at about 3.00 pm he had a short nap and then spent some time repainting the interior of the house 43 Ford Lane, Crewe, which he was in the process of buying, before going to bed at 7.45 pm. The next day an early turn again found Lockwood, the shedman, calling at his house at about 1.45 am. When he booked on at Crewe North an hour later, J. Hallmark, the running shift foreman, told him he was to work the overnight sleeping car train from Perth forward to London Euston, in place of the regular driver who was on leave, and return with the 8.30 pm down Special Travelling Postal Office, presumably after lodging at Camden. At Crewe the engine Stanier '8P' 'Duchess' class No. 46242 *City of Glasgow*, of Camden, had been prepared on shed by others after its trip down from London with 7.20 pm the 'Royal Highlander' sleeping car train from Euston, thereby leaving more than adequate time for him to read the notices and then oil round his engine before leaving shed at about 3.45 am. His mate on this occasion was the regular link 23-year-old fireman Colin Turnock of Wistaston near Crewe, who had joined the railway as a bar boy in 1943. He had graduated to cleaner the next year and been appointed fireman the year after that at the age of 16. Following his return from military service in 1949, he had regularly fired on trips to London with express passenger trains.

It was a foggy night and movements around the Crewe complex had become delayed and Jones is said to have remarked that he had had difficulty reversing up to the Perth train standing at the platform. It had been due to arrive at Crewe at 4.02 am, but was 13 minutes late, and was allowed 16 minutes there for station work and for changing the engines. While Jones was waiting in the platform at Crewe station, he exchanged banter with his friend and fellow driver J. Hampton about the fog and his fireman's recent marriage. The guard, J. Kent of Carlisle, advised him that the train consisted of 11 vehicles weighing 364 tons, which will have included four sleeping cars, three of which were 12-wheelers, and three bogie vans, and that additional special stops were to be made at Nuneaton and Rugby. During this period, Jones' train was overtaken on the through road by driver F.B. Halliburton and fireman J. Parkinson, both of Carlisle Upperby shed, with the 14-coach 10.20 pm sleeping car train from Glasgow Central to Euston. They had had clear weather on their way south as far as Wigan, but from here on in foggy conditions had been encountered for virtually all the rest of the journey until Willesden, when the sun had appeared. Halliburton is reported to have said that, although this had been some of the worst conditions he had encountered for some time, he had had no real difficulty observing his signals.

The Glasgow train had been checked by signals at Bletchley, overtook the 7.31 am nine-coach local train from Tring on the up slow line at Aspley and had to slow down for a 15 mph temporary speed restriction through Watford tunnel, but soon recovered speed again. Speed was put on a bit to enable water to be picked up from Bushey troughs and Halliburton was positive that he saw Harrow No. 1 up fast colour light distant signals before they sailed through Harrow & Wealdstone station at 55 to 60 mph at 8.08 am, 93 minutes late. The local train from Tring was hauled by a Fowler 2-6-4T driven by 53-year-old A.W. Payne of St Georges Road, Watford and fired by A.R. Hine aged 20 years, of Thorpe Crescent, Oxhey, both based at Watford shed.

At 4.37 am, 19 minutes after the Glasgow train had passed through Crewe, driver Jones with the Perth train carrying 90 passengers, set off 32 minutes late. Despite the continuing fog and being slowed for signals at Baddesley and Atherstone, as well as the special stops at Nuneaton and Rugby, the Perth train had all but caught up with the Glasgow train, as a consequence of which they were brought to a stand at Watford Tunnel (North End) for two minutes. Clearing the speed restriction through the tunnel and with the signals off through Watford Junction resuming speed the weather improved. Near Headstone Lane, now about 80 minutes late, they passed the 4.32 am freight train of 58 empty wagons from Norwood (Southern Region) to Northampton travelling in the opposite direction on the down slow line. This had left Willesden at 7.25 am hauled by an eight-coupled goods engine driven by R.C. Brown from Willesden shed and had been stopped two or three times on the way. It was this train that at Harrow had to pass before signalman Alf Armitage in Harrow No. 1 signal box could set the road for the local train to cross, as scheduled, to the up fast line and stop at platform 4 of Harrow & Wealdstone station to pick up many more passengers waiting to board.

For reasons that have never been satisfactorily explained driver Jones, of the Perth train, appeared not to have seen the Harrow No. 1 up fast distant colour light which must have been displaying yellow to protect the local train, now heavily loaded with commuters, standing at the platform, and therefore failed to apply his train's brakes in preparation to bringing it to a stand at the up fast outer home, 628 yards to the rear of the local train. Instead he appears to have only seen the adverse semaphore home of this signal, or possibly even only the inner fast home 188 yards from the local, at the last moment. This of course was far too late: his train collided violently into the rear of the crowded local at about 50 to 55 mph. Even worse, in ploughing through the rear coaches, his engine was deflected to the right, thereby fouling the down fast line just as the double-headed 8.00 am ex-Euston express train for Liverpool and Manchester was passing through the station.

The first of the two trains involved in the initial collision was the 7.31 am up local passenger train from Tring to Euston carrying about 800 commuters mainly bound for London, made up of nine non-corridor bogie coaches hauled by a '4MT' Fowler 2-6-4 tank engine No. 42389, which was being driven from the right-hand side as it was running bunker first. The train was more heavily loaded than usual, because the following one had been cancelled as part of revised services introduced during work on a £300,000 scheme for the installation of colour light signalling and associated simplification of track work at Euston. This train was one of a series which were run on weekday mornings to Euston from the residential area in the Chilterns. It was booked to stop at all stations to Watford inclusive, due to leave there at 8.01 am to arrive at Euston at 8.27 am after an intermediate stop at Harrow & Wealdstone from 8.10 to 8.12 am. The working timetable indicated that it was booked to run to Harrow No. 1 box on the up slow line and to continue from there to Euston on the fast line, so as to leave the slow line clear for empty stock movements from Willesden. Every endeavour was made to keep these commuter services on time. Other than in an emergency, the signalmen were expected to maintain the routeing specified, and give residential trains precedence over any late running night expresses from the North. The other train was the 8.15 pm overnight up express train from Perth to Euston, from Crewe hauled by No. 46242 *City of Glasgow*.

The third train, which ran into the wreckage of the first collision, was the Saturday-excepted limited load 8.00 am down express from Euston to Liverpool (Lime Street), with through coaches for Manchester (London Road), both portions being due to arrive at their destinations at 11.58 am. This train was the faster of two services to those two cities, with the first stop at Crewe due at 11.02 am and subsequent intermediate stop at Stockport only. This was scheduled to be followed by the 8.30 am from Euston calling at several of the more important towns on the way. On 8th October, 1952 the 8.00 am train consisted of 15 bogie

The leading locomotive of the Liverpool and Manchester train, No. 45637 *Windward Islands*. Here the engine is seen lying on its side partly across the double slip giving entry to the berthing sidings, as wisps of steam still escape from around the top feed pipes. Composite sleeping car No. M723M from the Perth train can be seen in the background, yet to be towed away largely undamaged.   *London Midland Region, BR*

vehicles, including four vans at the rear, and conveying 186 passengers. The leading four coaches were for Liverpool and would have been divided at Crewe with most of the remainder going on to Manchester, but with vans at the rear for Crewe, Holyhead and Glasgow. The crews of the third ingredient to this sorry saga were driver Albert Perkins and fireman George Cowper on the leading '6P' 'Jubilee' class locomotive No. 45637 *Windward Islands* piloting driver William H. Darton and fireman George Dowler, all from Edge Hill, in '8P' Pacific No. 46202 *Princess Anne*. No. 45637 had merely been attached in front as a means of working back to her home depot. Their departure had been delayed by five minutes due to brake problems. So, despite the 15-coach train, the two engines were beginning to recover lost time as they approached Harrow & Wealdstone station at about 50 mph on the down fast line. Further details of the marshalling of these trains will be found in *Appendix One*.

The local train, having travelled up until this point on the slow line, transferred as usual to the up fast line by means of a crossover at the country end of the station, and had stopped, as booked, at platform 4 on the up fast line. It had been standing there for about 1½ minutes. Its brakes had just been released prior to departure, when at 8.18½ am it was struck violently in the rear by the Perth express. Due to the interlocking of the frame in Harrow No. 1 signal box, the trailing points of the crossover from up slow to up fast were still locked in the reverse position by the up fast starting signal ahead which had been pulled off to authorise the local train to proceed on its journey, when the express had burst through them.

The engine of the Perth train, having ploughed through three of the rear coaches of the local train and derailed the fourth, slewed across the down fast line just as the (down) Liverpool express was approaching at not much less than 60 mph. Both of the Liverpool train engines were forced to the left across platform Nos. 2 and 3 by the obstruction and came to rest on their sides foul of the up electric line opposite Harrow No. 2 signal box. A direct short circuit of the traction current caused the isolators to be thrown, thereby cutting off all power to the conductor rails of the up electric line. Severe depressions in both rails (113 lb./yd flat bottomed) of the up fast line about five yards beyond the platform ramp indicated that a heavy vertical blow to the track must have occurred as the engine of the Perth train, No. 46242, plunged into the local train. The engine itself was found derailed to the right on to the down fast line, more or less upright, about 78 yards beyond the first point of impact *(Fig. 5, page 76)*. The tender was overturned to the left, and had crushed the left-hand side of the engine cab as it was slewed round almost at right angles to the tracks. From the very heavy damage sustained by the engine at the front, particularly at the right-hand side, it was evident that it had been in direct contact with the leading engine of the Liverpool train, which was correspondingly severely damaged. There was no means of knowing whether it was still moving forward at the time, but it is possible that it was stopped by the impact from penetrating into the sixth coach of the local train (fourth from the rear) with which it was found in close contact.

After No. 46242 *City of Glasgow* had been re-railed and placed in a siding, it was found that most of the motion parts had been torn away and the right-hand side of engine had nothing more left than twisted rods. The main frames were severely buckled, the front end of the right-hand frame plate was torn away from the inside cylinder casting, whilst the right-hand outside cylinder and steam chest were smashed. The crushing of the comparatively lightly constructed smoke box plating absorbed much energy, thereby saving the boiler from serious structural damage, though the front tube plate was bent. Three of the main steam pipes in the smoke box were broken. Steam pressure in the boiler must have been released immediately by the breaking off of one of the safety valves and a top feed clack box, whilst the displacing of a mud hole door on the firebox allowed the water to be blown away, with the result that the

The underframes and bogies to the leading coaches of the Liverpool/Manchester train were, on contact with the derailed Perth locomotive, ripped off and piled up to form a ramp up over which subsequent coaches of the train rode. On the right can be seen the eighth coach No. M30049, a kitchen car. *Anthony V. Gregory*

Beyond the open door a coach has ridden up to demolish the span of the station footbridge over the fast lines. On the right the door of the ninth vehicle in the Liverpool/Manchester train, No. M7465M, a restaurant first open, stands ajar, all able-bodied passengers and restaurant staff having long since left. Just prior to the accident Arthur E. Arnold, Manager of Wyman's bookstall, went to retrieve a paper that had blown onto the platform and stood dumbfounded as debris fell around him, yet he remained unscathed. *Anthony V. Gregory*

crown sheet was burnt. None of the steam joints in the cab was broken and the two water gauge glasses were intact, but the drain pipe and cock to the left-hand water gauge had been torn away, which must have released some steam and hot water. There was extensive damage to the tender, included the buckling of both the main frames and the bursting of the tank, resulting in the loss of all the feed water.

The sudden stopping and derailment of the heavy engine of the Perth train caused the leading two vans, an ex-GW 'Siphon G' and a passenger brake van, together with the following three passenger corridor coaches, Nos. M1799M, M26896M and M4469M, to pile up behind and above it. Their distorted underframes and bogies, together with some of the bogies of the local train, were compressed into a mass of wreckage about 100 ft long covering the up and down fast lines between platform Nos. 3 and 4. None of the carriage bodies was recognisable as such, and it may well be that their destruction was completed as some of the leading coaches of the Liverpool train rode over them. Severe damage to the Perth train stopped short behind the fifth coach. Damage to its sixth coach, No. M1517M, was little more than superficial and only its leading bogie was derailed. The four sleeping cars marshalled seventh to tenth and the brake van at the rear remained on the rails intact, apart from some displacement of internal fittings.

The pilot locomotive of the down Liverpool train, No. 45637 *Windward Islands*, was deflected to the left by the engine of the Perth train, as it passed under the station footbridge No. 43, and resulted in it ploughing its way across

THE ACCIDENT

platform Nos. 2 and 3 between the down fast and the up electric lines, coming to rest on its left-hand side across the electric lines at an angle of about 30°, approximately 75 yards from the point of impact. This was followed by the train locomotive, No. 46202 *Princess Anne*, which overturned to the left partly on the further edge of the platform.

Apart from the boiler, *Windward Islands* was reduced to virtual scrap. The bogie was wrecked and its component parts scattered, whilst the buffer beam and the frames were folded back as far as the leading coupled wheels and had to be cut away before the remains of the engine could be recovered. All three cylinder castings were smashed, and the rim of the right-hand leading coupled wheel was broken off its centre, which itself was fractured in several places. There was also very heavy damage at the rear end as the tender with the rest of the train behind it had driven into it. The tender tank was torn from the underframe and turned upside down, whilst one of the distorted side frame plates was later found beneath engine No. 46202 as it lay on its side.

The structural and other damage to *Princess Anne* was also severe and extensive. The main frames were buckled and the bogie centre pivot casting fractured and the frame of the rear carrying truck was also broken. The tender, which had remained coupled to the overturned engine, was more or less upright on its wheels on the remains of the platform. There was heavy damage at the rear, presumably as the leading coach had been forced against it by the momentum of the train behind, and its main frames were buckled.

The leading corridor brake third of the Liverpool train, No. M26856M, followed the two engines to the left on to the down fast platform with its bogies still below the underframe. The right-hand side of its body was ripped out by the underframe of the following corridor composite coach, No M4813M, the body of which was destroyed. The remains of the underframe and body of the third coach, a first class corridor No. M1124M, were on the down fast platform alongside the leading brake third. In contrast, the fourth coach, No. M34108 a corridor brake third, rode diagonally to the right across the wreckage of the Perth train and came to rest on the up fast platform.

Unlike most of the other coaches, this was an all-steel coach of British Railways standard design and although its underframe was only slightly distorted, the majority of its roof at the rear was torn away and left behind as it was forced upward against the footbridge girders. The brake and luggage compartments at the rear were wrecked and the front end crumpled, but it had not disintegrated, leaving the partitions of the four passenger compartments in place. This and the other BR-designed coaches, like most former LNER and Southern Railway corridor coaches, were fitted with the buck-eye coupling, instead of the screw coupling still used by the LMS, and, if coupled to other vehicles similarly equipped, should have prevented telescoping of the coaches when involved in a collision such as this. Nonetheless, the potential benefit of this safety feature was negated when, as in this case, such coaches were used individually and randomly dispersed amongst coaches not so fitted.

The fifth coach of the Liverpool train, No. M24683M, a corridor composite was one of the last designs of LMS coach and also had a steel body shell. Nonetheless, it was demolished and its twisted underframe lay on the pile of

A mass of metal work, consisting of more carriage underframes and bogies, supports a pyramid of wreckage around the footbridge. *Anthony V. Gregory*

bogies close to the footbridge, but the sixth and seventh, Nos. M34287 and M27266M, continued on a straight course mounting the engine of the Perth train and the other wreckage on the alignment of the down fast line. No. M34287, another all-steel coach of the new BR standard design, suffered a good deal less damage than the others; its underframe and body shell kept their shape well and, even though there was a good deal of internal damage, all the compartments could be identified. On the other hand the sheeted steel on timber frame body sides of No. M27266M behind it, was torn from the underframe and ended up directly above the buried engine of the Perth train, with its roof reaching to a height of about 30 ft above rail level.

The leading end of the next coach, kitchen car No. M30049, ended up resting on a number of bogies torn from previous vehicles causing it to be wedged up under the footbridge, but with its trailing bogie still on the rails. The front end of its body was driven in, although structural damage to the underframe was not very severe. All the gas for cooking was discharged to atmosphere as the reservoirs were punctured, but fortunately this did not catch fire. There was no serious structural damage to the undergear or bodywork of any of the remaining seven vehicles behind the kitchen car and, except for the leading bogie of the ninth coach, all their wheels remained on the track. As the third train collided with the wreckage of the first two, the ever increasing number of derailed coaches at some point struck the underside of the footbridge girders eventually peeling back the main girder on its country side.

The damage to the locomotives of three express trains and the destruction of rolling stock caused by the two collisions at high speed were altogether exceptional, the debris completely burying the engine of the Perth train as it lay

The upward thrust of the coaches of the Liverpool/Manchester train riding up on top of the wreckage from the collision between the Perth and local trains, forced them through the floor of the station footbridge. Here a tangled mass of coach underframes and bogies, together with the odd compartment partition, lie among the twisted structural steelwork and decking of the footbridge.
Anthony V. Gregory

Beyond the footbridge the remains of the second, third and fifth coaches of the Liverpool/Manchester train reached to a similar height. Note the buffer-head thrust through the porthole window of the fifth coach, No. M24683M.   *Anthony V. Gregory*

foul of the down fast line. Thirteen vehicles were compressed into a compact heap of wreckage about 54 feet wide by 135 feet long and 30 feet high. Leaving aside re-railed coaches which could subsequently be towed away, the total weight of debris arising from three locomotives and 16 coaches to be removed amounted to approximately 1,000 tons, to which must be added the span of the station footbridge, a certain amount of the platform canopy and dislodged masonry of the platform wall. All in all this required 200 wagons to cart away.

Initial Reaction of Railway Staff

Relief signalman Alf Armitage in Harrow No. 1 signal box, despite having done all the right things, as the subsequent official inquiry was to show, instead of going into a state of panic, once he realised a collision was inevitable, first pulled the lever in his frame used to place detonators on the up fast line. Although the locomotive of the Perth train exploded these, it was already too close to the local train to prevent the collision or alert the driver to brake soon enough to reduce measurably the speed upon impact. Once this had occurred, realising that he had recently accepted the Liverpool/Manchester train on the adjacent down fast line and that this was now imminent, he immediately reversed the down fast home signal as it bore down on the obstruction caused by the first collision, but again too late to prevent a second. With these two emergency actions carried out, it remained for him to send 'obstruction danger' on all four lines under his control, the up and down fast and slow lines to the adjacent signal boxes, Hatch End to the north and Wembley North to the south.

Prompt action by the signalman of Harrow No. 2 box led to the power being cut off from the up and down electric line as well between Kenton and Harrow sub-stations at 8.23 am. As a result an up electric train from Watford Junction, which had just left Harrow station, was stopped well clear, reinforced by the automatic reversal of the up line home signal to danger.

The guard of the local train, Billy Merritt, on seeing and hearing the Perth train approaching at speed, jumped down onto the track and took cover under the coping of the platform of the down slow line, waiting there until the noise of the second collision had died down. After that he went to the signal box and was assured by Armitage that all lines were protected.

To J. Kent, the guard from Crewe of the Perth train, the first indication that something was wrong was a severe application of the brake, during which he noticed that vacuum gauge in his van had dropped almost instantaneously to zero. A short interval of perhaps five seconds later, he felt three violent lurches forward, followed immediately by an equally violent rebound. From this he concluded that the driver had spotted something just too late. As he was not injured, his thoughts were to protect the rear of his train, so he got down with a red flag and detonators with the intention of placing these in the up fast line, but, as he was quite close to the signal box, he went there first. Here he found the signalman appeared to 'have had a shaking', but was told by him that all lines had been protected, so he went round to the offside to check for any obstruction of the down fast line, only to find that the Liverpool train had already run into the wreckage.

Travelling in the fifth coach of the local train were several senior railwaymen, including Frederick Abraham, the Regional Motive Power Superintendent and Stanley Williams, the Signal and Telecommunications Engineer of the London Midland Region. Although their compartments had been damaged in the accident, these gentlemen soon sized up the situation and set about organising the relief and subsequent restoration of services. Following the accident they both immediately went to the signal box to ascertain the situation there. Mr Williams noted the indication on the block instruments and the position of the levers in the frame, while Mr Abraham used the railway telephone to set in motion the railway's rescue and recovery operations. Mr Williams then instructed telegraph lineman C. Thorpe to go back on foot and check the aspect of the up fast distant signal. About half an hour later Thorpe found both distant signals displaying yellow aspects, indicating caution. When he got back to the box he tested the up fast berth track circuit annunciator buzzer and found it in working order.

Having made sure the emergency services had been summoned, Mr C.S. Rolinson, the station master, made his way to the signal box to satisfy himself that the obstruction danger signal had been sent to the adjacent signal boxes for all four lines, after which he signed the register at 8.28 am. He found signalman Armitage in a severe state of shock, his face deathly white and very upset, so he assisted him out of the box to give him some fresh air by sitting on the steps for a while. After that Mr Rolinson occupied himself with the rescue work.

Likewise, Mr R.W. Hall, a traffic apprentice aged 26, who was also in the local train, went to the signal box about 18 minutes after the accident as Mr Rolinson was returning to the station platform. He confirmed the position of the levers as Mr Williams had stated and signalman Armitage's condition.

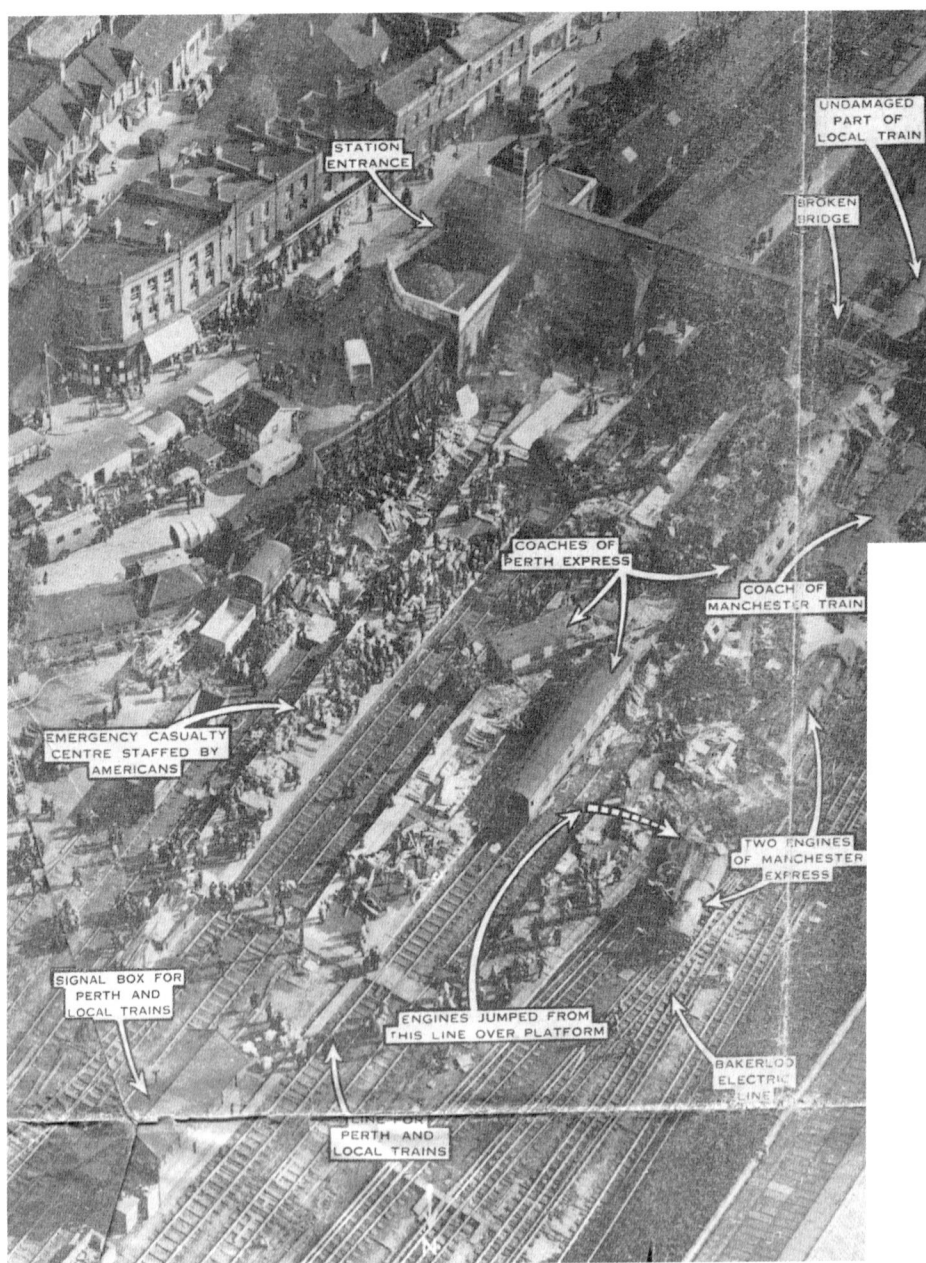

A picture carried the next morning in *The Daily Telegraph and Morning Post* newspaper depicting the scene of devastation from the air and with the various features of the double collision annotated. *Author's Collection*

Chapter Four

The Response

Press Activities

The Metropolitan Police Information Room advised their Press Bureau at 8.25 am that a serious railway accident had occurred and they in turn informed the Press Association and Exchange Telegraph with the result that news of the accident was mentioned on the BBC's 9 o'clock (radio) News and included an appeal for doctors, nurses and qualified first aid personnel to go to the scene. The Metropolitan Police also sent two press officers from the Commissioner's Office to Wealdstone Police station to gather information direct and to handle the anticipated enquiries from the press on the spot.

By 8.34 am the Public Relations Officer of the London Midland Region in London, George Dow, was informed of the accident. Obviously news of such importance resulted in a large number of telephone calls from the newspapers and for a time the lines will have been busy and those able to answer such calls fully stretched. As a consequence, and because it was thought for a time that a tube train was involved, London Transport's Press Office helped out by fielding a number of enquiries from the Press Association, the London evening papers and the BBC. Within 45 minutes, however, Dow and his staff had set up a reporters' room at Euston House from where the press was kept informed. As a result the manner in which the press was handled throughout the event and its aftermath was much appreciated by the newspaper industry.

That these facilities were utilised, is exemplified by the extensive coverage given to the event in all the national dailies and local papers. Press photographers visited the site for at least the next three days and the BBC even diverted an outside television broadcast team intended for the horse racing at Ascot to record the scene at the site of the accident arriving at 12 noon. At 11.15 am the police at Harrow Police station were advised by the Ministry of Aviation by telephone that they had specially granted permission for two aircraft belonging to Morton's Air Services to fly over the site at low level with a party of press photographers and this information was passed on to the site. However, around noon, despite some smoke and haze arising from the scene, several other low flying aircraft were observed. Their identification letters were therefore duly noted by the police and the Air Traffic Control Centre at Uxbridge asked to recall the aircraft. On landing the pilots were warned that the police had taken their identification numbers and might initiate proceedings against them. Undaunted, however, further aircraft were spotted flying low over the scene during the afternoon. A report together with police witness statements were submitted to the Treasury Solicitor, who deferred from taking legal proceedings and suggested instead that cautionary letters be sent to those implicated.

Mounting of the Rescue Operation

It was inevitable that the casualty list would be substantial, particularly as the local train was crowded and many of the coach bodies were of wood, which like Nelson's warships, can enhance the risk of injury due to flying splinters. Ninety-eight passengers, together with four railway employees on duty, were killed outright in the accident, while 10 passengers later died in hospital, giving a total of 112, the second highest number of deaths in a railway accident in the British Isles. Of these, it was established that 64 passengers had travelled in the local train from Tring, 23 in the overnight train from Perth and seven in the morning express to Liverpool and Manchester, while the train in which 14 dead had been travelling, or indeed possibly standing on the platform or crossing the footbridge, could not be determined with certainty. Some 167 passengers were taken to hospital for treatment, of whom 10 subsequently succumbed, with 84 detained overnight, plus four railway servants, including the fireman of the leading engine of the Liverpool train and the driver and fireman of the second engine; all three having made remarkable escapes when their locomotives overturned. By the end of the month of October 40 people were still in hospital, whilst at the close of the year 12 remained, including five members of staff, reportedly progressing favourably. Over and above these, 183 people suffering minor injury or shock were treated on site and in some cases subsequently made their own way to hospitals local to their homes or place of work. A substantial number of the passengers in the local train had boarded at Watford Junction, many having entered the station at the country end by means of the access off the Callowlands Road bridge, now removed, and therefore travelling in the rear of the train. This meant that a high proportion of the casualties came from the community of north Watford. Many were railwaymen on their way to work in London, mostly in the London Midland Region offices at Euston. Among the casualties, 36 of those who lost their lives, 57 detained in hospital and 57 of the less severely injured who attended hospital were railway employees.

Very soon after the accident occurred, 16 telephone calls were made to summon assistance, initially at 8.19 am by a porter on the platform, followed a minute later by the station master C.S. Rolinson and others, whilst police sergeant 39'X' Morgan, warrant officer at Wealdstone magistrates court, witnessed the accident as he stepped off a No. 230 bus outside the station. He immediately ran the 300 yards to Wealdstone police station, where he informed the station officer, Police Sergeant 113'X' Gaskell. As a consequence the Metropolitan Police Information Room was promptly able to mobilise their resources and to advise the Middlesex Fire and Ambulance Service, with the result that all the local emergency services arrived on the scene very soon. Railway staff, who were working at or in the vicinity of the station, together with railwaymen in the trains or on the platform and other uninjured passengers also made an immediate start on the work of first-aid and rescue. Leslie Rowlands, of the Operating Superintendent's Department at Euston, who had been in the fourth coach from the rear of the local train and, although severely shaken, took a major part in organising these efforts, including making sure that all railway departments were promptly notified of the accident.

Medical Assistance

The first ambulance and doctor arrived at 8.22 am, within three minutes of the collision, and the Police and the first fire engine at about the same time. From then on, a string of ambulances, doctors, nurses, additional fire engines and police arrived in increasing numbers, together with a medical unit of the United States Air Force (USAF), who rendered valuable service. Police cars toured the neighbourhood to collect doctors and convey them to the scene. The doctors who responded by attending included Allen; Kamer Das; Harrison; J.S. Lindsey; Florence O'Sullivan, the first British doctor on the scene; T.D. Renwick; Charles R.D. Porter; R. Tudor Edwards; L.K. Wills; M.E. Winters and H. Wolmuth. An emergency casualty station was set up in the open on platforms 6 and 7 and mattresses from the sleeping cars of the Perth train used as hospital beds, whilst a casualty clearing post was located in the yard adjacent to the goods shed. As well as manning the first aid post, by 9.30 am sufficient doctors were on hand to enable one to be placed with each rescue group working on and in the wreckage. They were able to administer pain relieving drugs, mainly in the form of morphine or pethadine, and where necessary certify death, thus enabling the rescue group leader to redirect the team's efforts to where lives might yet be saved. In this connection a temporary mortuary was set up in a local community hall to allow the ambulances to concentrate on conveying the injured to hospital. Later, as many of the casualties had been removed, some of the doctors working with the rescue groups were redirected to the local hospitals to provide additional assistance there. Some persons were freed by amputation of crushed limbs, using the emergency medical boxes carried in some of the ambulances. The Royal Air Force was also there under the direction of Squadron Leader D.G. Bonham, the Senior Medical Officer at RAF Stanmore, and his medical orderlies crawled amongst the wreckage to inject morphine in the injured, whilst other airman carried out rescue work and members of the Women's Royal Air Corps provided for the welfare of all concerned by serving tea.

Once the more easily extracted cases were retrieved, the rescue effort slowed down as heavier pieces of debris were removed, mainly still by hand or improvised hand tools, to afford access to those trapped more deeply in the wreckage. The greatest of care was necessary in carrying out these operations to avoid the risk of causing parts of the wreckage to move, slip or collapse on the casualty. In many cases a doctor or other suitable person had to remain with the patient perhaps until the appropriate tool could be brought to their location, during which time conversation with them was maintained to keep up their morale and remind them that they were not forgotten. Once heavy jacks arrived, it became possible to raise the side of a coach and thus enable access to be gained for the removal of a substantial amount of debris trapping a number of further casualties. The carrying away of the footbridge span over the main lines added to the chaos. Rescue operations were not helped when at 3.25 pm a small fire broke out in the wreckage, but this was quickly extinguished by the firemen in attendance.

At 1.10 pm, and again later, all work was briefly halted and silence called for, to establish whether sounds could be heard from any of the injured still trapped.

United States Air Force medical teams in the emergency casualty station set up on platform Nos. 6 and 7, poised ready to attend to the injured as they are extracted from the wreckage.
Anthony V. Gregory

Among the American Air Force medical team was Lieutenant Abbie Sweetwine from their base at South Ruislip. She was seized upon by the British press as the 'Angel of Platform 5', as she and her colleagues rendered more than just first aid to the injured, but stabilised their condition on site and arranged for their removal to hospital in order of seriousness of their condition. She is seen here taking a break with a sergeant.
Anthony V. Gregory

THE RESPONSE 37

Two further seriously injured cases were removed at 2.30 pm; by 3.30 pm it was realised that most living casualties had been removed and by 1.30 am, early the next day, it was clear there was little chance of anyone now being found alive in the wreckage. With the removal of the last body, the railway authorities finally declared the end of rescue operations at 12.17 pm on Saturday 11th October, thus allowing the withdrawal of the fire brigade, ambulance service, civil defence rescue squads and police public address system.

The American Air Force Contribution

Much was made in the national newspapers at the time of the contribution made by the American medical teams from 3rd and 7th USAF based at Victoria Road, South Ruislip. This came about because some Americans were caught up in the accident, four of whom lost their lives at least two being a servicemen and his wife. A surviving US serviceman informed their airbase at Ruislip. Their response was to send two officers to the scene who, arriving at 9.40 am and on seeing the devastation, offered the services of a mobile first-aid post, which was accepted, so that by 10.15 am some personnel were on the scene and at work. They also alerted their neighbouring bases at West Drayton and Bushy Park, Teddington and together assembled a team under Lieutenant Colonel Weideman amounting to 85 men and women, including eight doctors, three of whom were among their top surgeons in Europe, experienced in performing emergency operations, and 30 military police and maintenance staff. Around 11.30 am they arrived in six ambulances, together with staff cars and trucks which brought portable dispensaries with supplies of morphine, blood plasma, stretchers and splints. A local doctor, R. Tudor Edwards, is reported to have commented: 'They worked magnificently and their organisation was first class. They gave intravenous plasma and this without doubt helped in preventing delayed shock and must have resulted in saving many lives'. Their main contribution, however, lay in the manner in which they applied their expertise to the recovery of the injured by bringing hospital treatment to the patient right beside the wreckage at the railway station, such as the application of drips, rather than their treatment being delayed by the journey to hospital. Such was the demand that Colonel Eugene Coler, Chief Air Surgeon of 7th United States Air Division arranged for further supplies of blood plasma and morphia to be flown from as far away as Burtonwood in Lancashire to Northolt. At the emergency casualty station, teams of one doctor and three airmen worked among the injured, offering first aid treatment and setting simple fractures. The newspapers' darling was Lieutenant Abbie Sweetwine, who, during the hectic process of moving the injured through and on to hospital, used her lipstick to mark 'MS' on the patient's forehead to indicate that morphine sulphate had already been administered and that therefore a further dose too soon would be dangerous. At midday a chuck wagon (mobile canteen) arrived from their base at South Ruislip bringing coffee, doughnuts and sandwiches to feed to rescue workers. Although Lt Col Weidman was advised by Mr S.G. Hearn, Operating Superintendent LMR, that they were relieved of their duties at 4.45 pm, they apparently remained thereafter for some considerable time.

USAF staff stand around their mobile 'chuck wagon' standing in the goods yard to provide refreshment to their men and others. *Anthony V. Gregory*

Casualties and their Removal

The Middlesex Fire Service County Control, at County headquarters, Pinner Road, North Harrow, received news of the disaster by an emergency telephone call at 8.19 am. In the days before wailing sirens fitted to emergency service vehicles, other road users were persuaded to make way for police cars, fire engines and ambulances by the frantic ringing of their bells. Appliances and ambulances were immediately directed to the railway station from both Wealdstone and Pinner fire stations, the first fire engine arriving at 8.30 am. By 8.36 am, once the seriousness of the crash became apparent, nearby hospitals, the coroner's officers and mortuary staff were all alerted, whilst ambulances and men from all the surrounding area were summoned to help with rescue work.

As well as the police and fire services called to the scene of the accident, passengers in the three trains or already on the platform not actually injured, together with general members of the public in the vicinity of the station, rushed to volunteer to assist in the rescue work. Their work with very meagre equipment, initially directed by the police, was largely carried out by hand. Parties were arranged, to carry out different aspects of the work, so that for each group working inside the wreckage, there was another available outside to pass on pieces of debris, the injured or the dead, all often requiring considerable double handling. The difficulty of access led to improvisation to secure the debris in order to afford access for the recovery of the injured. In some cases up to four groups would be involved in the chain from inside a deeply buried coach to a safe area. As sufficient professional resources became available, the Police cleared the site of unnecessary persons. This gave more room to manoeuvre during the work and space in which reserves of manpower could be held and relieved personnel to have a break and take refreshment.

With the arrival of the Deputy Chief Fire Officer of the Middlesex Fire Brigade management of these activities was taken over by him. He set up a control point in the office of the coal merchant Rogers Fuels near the main entrance to the station. Communications were directed from a radio vehicle positioned in the station yard and in contact with initially two, supplemented later by four more, 'walkie-talkie' sets and the county control room. The number of ambulances required was increased at 8.30 am to 10 and 10 minutes later to 20 with all other non-urgent ambulance work in the district frozen. By 9.00 am a temporary first aid post on the platform and temporary mortuary had been set up in the station goods yard. To the subsequent displeasure of his superiors, who thought he should have remained in his office, K.G. 'Tim' Ely, Ambulance Superintendent from No. 5 Depot at Kenton, having learnt of the alert from a passing policeman, mustered all available staff and vehicles and set off for the scene. On arrival he set up an ambulance control in Smith's Stationers opposite the station. He organised a casualty clearing station staffed by two doctors and a lady from the Women's Voluntary Service (WVS), whilst the ambulance loading point was brought into the yard from outside the front of the railway station. There he was to remain for the next three days. Most of the easily accessible casualties were extracted and dispatched to hospital for treatment within two hours; by 10.30 am the rate of recovery of the injured had slackened sufficiently to permit the number of ambulances to be reduced to 10

Access to retrieve the injured involved working amongst the piles of wreckage, crawling between carriage roofs, sides, floors, compartment partitions and seats etc., to burrow down to reach those casualties buried beneath. Here a fireman, ambulancemen, an RAF sergeant and others are attempting to place a victim onto a stretcher. *Anthony V. Gregory*

The rescue operation gets underway amongst the heap of wreckage. American servicemen from bases at South Ruislip and Bushy are in evidence on platform 5 on the left, as they mingle with police, fireman and other rescuers, providing medical aid to the injured. In the foreground a casualty recovered from the wreckage is carried away. *Metropolitan Police Museum*

THE RESPONSE

and at 3.00 pm to five. The six radio sets were of great assistance at the beginning of rescue operations and, as the batteries of those belonging to the fire service became flat, others sets were loaned by the police. The 'walkie-talkie' sets enabled senior officers in charge of operations to direct stretchers and medical assistance where they were most urgently needed.

During Wednesday there were 95 firemen working amongst the wreckage supplemented by 35 recruits from the Fire Service Training School at Finchley, to gain valuable experience and as a disciplined labour force to work with and support the more experienced fireman already there. The Assistant Chief Officer of Middlesex was in charge, assisted by other senior officers, whilst the Chief Officer, Mr Alf Wooder, was also present part of the time. Eight fire appliances were called. Two emergency tenders were also sent containing two standard and two portable acetylene sets for cutting metalwork, hack saws, crowbars and other rescue equipment. Both fire and ambulance staff personnel were relieved at four to five hour intervals. Two or three fire pumps remained over Wednesday and Thursday nights, in case fire broke out during the continuing rescue and clearing up operations, manned by the Auxiliary Fire Service, these eventually being stood down at 12.30 am on Saturday 11th October.

Immediately following the accident, clouds of steam escaping from the locomotives tended to obscure the scene. There were, however, only a few minor fires in the wreckage caused by flue gases from locomotive chimneys and burning coals from the crashed engines, which the fire brigade soon extinguished before any became at all serious. The firemen then dealt with escaping gas and with water pouring from a main which was burst as a result of the impact. Thereafter their hoses were kept charged with water so as to be able quickly to extinguish any small fires that might be caused by sparks arising from oxy-acetylene torches cutting up the wreckage. These hoses were also useful in replenishing the water supplies to locomotives and steam cranes which could not readily reach water columns during their prolonged periods on site. After helping the first of the injured to safety, the firemen systematically searched the wreckage for victims before cranes were allowed to move any pieces of debris. On the down fast line it was found that the wreckage had ended up in such a way that it was possible to shore up a passage from the country end and crawl in beside the platform wall and reach some of the dead and severely wounded in the local train.

The nearest hospitals of Harrow Cottage, Wembley and Willesden General could not on their own cope with the large number of casualties. Instead the greatest number were dealt with by Edgware General Hospital, with others conveyed to Central Middlesex, and as far as Mount Vernon, Northwood, and Watford Peace Memorial hospitals, whilst certain cases were transferred to Royal Orthopaedic Hospital at Stanmore.

Casualties Handled by Hospitals	Admitted	Treated and sent home
Edgware General	54	49
Willesden General	2	4
Harrow Cottage	12	21
Wembley	11	4
Central Middlesex, Willesden	9	4
Watford, Peace Memorial	2	9
Stanmore, Royal National Orthopaedic	3	0
Mount Vernon, Northwood	4	0

The cab of No. 46537 *Windward Islands* is seen to be badly stove in, while the tender body has separated from the underframe and overturned. Although injured, the fireman of this engine, together with both the driver and fireman of the following engine, miraculously escaped with their lives.
Anthony V. Gregory

A close up of the leading coach of the Liverpool and Manchester train which has followed the engines on to platforms 2 and 3, while the sixth coach with others carried straight on to end up on top of the debris, resulting from the first collision between the Perth and the local trains.
Metropolitan Police Museum

Stretchers, together with mattresses retrieved from the sleeping cars of the Perth train, were laid out in rows on the rails of the sidings beside the goods shed, with nurses and ambulances in attendance, as a man walks by with a heavy jack on his shoulders. Just as well it was not raining!
Metropolitan Police Museum

In the foreground is the emergency casualty station set up on platforms 6 and 7. The breakdown train from Rugby arrived at 1.25 pm and by early afternoon its 30 ton Cowans Sheldon steam crane No. RS1075/30 was at work standing on the up slow line. Here the jib is raised ready to assist the swarm of rescuers standing on the pile of wreckage by very carefully lifting off small items.
Anthony V. Gregory

The remnants of one of the girders to the station footbridge, carried away by the force of impact of the coaches from the Liverpool and Manchester train, as they rose up over the engine of the Perth train, lie in the foreground on top of the debris. *Metropolitan Police Museum*

One of the first tasks of the fire brigade was to suppress any fires. Here one fireman has passed a hose into the debris behind the first coach of the Liverpool train, No. M26856M, while in the shadows the boot of another can be seen as he searches for signs of any conflagration.
Anthony V. Gregory

Rescuers scramble over and wriggle into the wreckage of demolished coaches in search of any more trapped passengers, whilst others manhandle a stretcher over an upturned coach roof. The coach bodies were largely constructed of either thin steel panels on wooden frames or fully wooden bodies, with only a few of all-steel construction. *Metropolitan Police Museum*

The second locomotive of the Liverpool train, No. 46202 *Princess Anne*, is seen lying on its side amongst the rubble of the platform it has just ploughed through. Behind it rescuers stand around the leading coach, a BR/LMR 'port-hole stock' brake corridor third No. M26856M, against which a ladder has been placed to gain access to the pile of coaches beyond.
Anthony V. Gregory

At Edgware General Hospital, 40 doctors, 250 nurses and four operating theatres were allocated to the task of caring for and treating the injured. To enable such resources to be mobilised, night staff remained on duty until late in the afternoon and 50 nurses due to take examinations were recalled to duty. During the afternoon Mr J.W. Watkins, Chief Regional Officer of the LMR and Mr A.G. Hamnett, Commercial Superintendent, made visits to several of these hospitals to express their sympathy and offer practical assistance where possible.

The bodies of the deceased were taken either from the scene or from the hospitals to a number of mortuaries in the area, as shown below:

Disposition of the Deceased

Mortuary	Number
Edgware General Hospital	33
Wealdstone	30
Kilburn	28
Hendon Town Hall	21

Ambulance Work

The initial response of the rescue services was met by sending four ambulances, together with two equipped with emergency medical boxes, two pump escape engines and one emergency tender fire engine. The first ambulance carrying injured persons left the station at 8.27 am and thereafter a continuous stream were on their way to the hospitals. At the peak, 21 ambulances were shuttling back and forth between the station and the hospitals, including three ambulances and three ambulance coaches from London County Council, and two ambulances from Edgware General Hospital.

Because those who had suffered least were able to abstract themselves from the wreckage on their own, or with a little help from other passengers or the first rescuers, it was the lightly injured who initially presented themselves for transport to hospital, when perhaps ambulance staff should have been seeking out and tending the more seriously hurt. People with minor injuries were packed in the vehicles, standing beside the more serious cases on stretchers and at one point the dazed and walking injured so swamped the available ambulances that the Police information room asked London Transport to send three buses and London County Council for three ambulances, but none showed up. Instead, a number of vehicles were commandeered by the Police, including a double-decker bus together with vans owned by the Royal Arsenal Co-operative Society and Jim Candey Ltd, to take them all to hospital. At times the supplies of stretchers and blankets became so low that the assistance of the London County Council was sought. Even so, resort was made to pole and canvas stretchers which at least had the advantage that the soiled canvas could be quickly changed between patients. At about 11.45 am, once the initial emergency of rushing casualties to hospital was over, the normal ambulance service in the county was resumed. By 12.15 pm the great majority of the injured had received first-aid attention and had been taken on to hospital. Seventy-nine bodies were removed to mortuaries on Wednesday. The Fire and Ambulance Service, nonetheless, remained on site until after the last body was removed and did not finally withdraw until 12.24 am on Sunday 12th October.

A stock-take following the operation, revealed that 12 rigid stretchers, one canvas stretcher and two blankets could not be accounted for, so an invoice for approximately £400 was sent to the Railway Executive. They initially declined to accept any responsibility, arguing that they had not been in control of this equipment, but in the end the issue was settled by the two parties equally shouldering the cost.

Police Activities

At Wealdstone police station Chief Inspector Ivan Bray took charge and notified his Chief Superintendent, sent calls for all local doctors and summoned the coroner's officers to attend the scene, before himself adjourning there. The accident occurred in No. 2 District of 'X' Division and the obvious need for large numbers of police officers led at 8.45 am to a radio message being sent from the wireless cars to the Information Room requesting reinforcements. These were drawn from three divisions (X, S and T) and based at such diverse stations as Acton, Hampstead, Hendon, Hounslow, Golder's Green, Ealing, Southall and Teddington, together with about 40 of those at the Hendon College Driving School four miles away.

The build up of police resources on the scene was rapid, to which must be added those retained back at the police stations to handle messages and enquiries, together with a number of off-duty officers living in the vicinity, who went to the station and offered their services.

	Build up of Police resources & doctors				
Rank/Item/Time	8.30 am	8.35 am	8.45 am	9.15 am	9.30 am
Chief Superintendent	-	-	-	1	1
Superintendent	-	-	-	-	1
Chief Inspector	1	1	1	1	1
Inspectors	-	1	1	2	3
Sergeants	2	4	6	8	16
Constables	10	18	28	52	115
Total police personnel	13	24	26	63	137
Wireless cars	3	3	5	9	12
General purpose cars	1	2	1	1	7
Motor-cycles	1	2	2	2	2
Van	-	1	1	1	1
Coach	-	-	-	-	1
Local doctors			2	18	18

Chief Superintendent David Illesley arrived at 9.05 am from Harrow Road police station to take charge of police operations and set up a Police Control Point on platform No. 7. By 9.30 am there were sufficient police resources available to enable a reserve force to be gathered at the Hendon District Garage. From here two inspectors, four sergeants, 50 constables on foot duty and 20 traffic officers and their cars were sent to Wealdstone police station to assist there from 2.00 pm, the remainder being released for other duties at 1.45 pm. At 9.45 am the request for further assistance was withdrawn, over 120 having arrived by 11.00 am. A mobile canteen to provide refreshments for this substantial force was requested but unfortunately due to the need to locate and stock such a vehicle, this did not arrive until about 4.00 pm, when it was located at Wealdstone police station until 6.00 am on 12th October. Those who had been on duty during the day were relieved as late turn personnel arrived with about 100 men of all ranks continuing work through the night. Despite the assistance of special constables who volunteered for duty, this was still more manpower than the division could muster on its own and the continuing level of assistance from other divisions is shown below and finally ceased at 10.00 pm on 11th October.

	Police manpower supplied by other divisions				
Date October	8/9	9	9/10	11	11
Shift	night	day	from 10.00 pm	day	from 2.00 pm
Inspectors	2	2	1	1	1
Sergeants	4	5	2	3	1
Constables	40	50	20	30	10

Amongst the railway police, all available uniformed and plain clothes officers at Euston were sent to the scene as soon as news of the accident came through. In due course, as railway police from other locations arrived on the scene, the Metropolitan Police Force was able by 4.30 pm to withdraw the majority of its members from within the railway premises, leaving only those manning the public address system, liaison with the ambulance service and a few CID officers for the protection of property.

Some police were placed on duty outside railway premises to control road traffic and public onlookers. To improve access to the station by ambulances and the vehicles of other emergency services, a traffic diversion was set up by the Police at 10.00 am, requiring a sergeant and 10 constables to implement. Wealdstone High Street/Station Road past the station was temporarily closed and traffic re-routed by way of Headstone Drive, Harrow View and College Road (southbound), or Hindes Road (northbound). Due to the limited headroom of 13 foot 6 inches under a bridge in Headstone Drive, however, buses and other high vehicles had to continue to use Station Road. Later the route was sign-posted by the Automobile Association. This diversion remained in place, apart from 10.00 pm to 6.00 am overnight, until noon on Friday 10th October. Sightseers peering over the boundary fences in the vicinity of the station tended to block the footway and were moved on. By the evening, as more spectators arrived, a considerable body of police officers and cars equipped with loudspeakers had to be deployed.

In the days before mobile phones and at a time when an Army 'walkie talkie' radio consisted of a large heavy back pack, the wireless (radio) in police patrol cars initially was the preferred means of communications until the GPO Telephones laid on temporary telephone lines for the use of the police. On the station site from 10.25 am onwards communications between doctors and rescue workers were assisted by the provision of a public address system installed by the Police. Amongst other things, this system was used to locate people who had escaped injury in the accident and who were now being sought by the casualty enquiry offices, but in the meantime had joined in the rescue effort.

From about 9.00 am Chief Inspector Richardson arrived to direct the work of CID officers undertaking the protection of property. For this purpose officers were positioned at strategic locations throughout the site, including the luggage vans containing mail and undamaged parts of the train, to receive recovered personal items and to prevent looting. This was just as well because, unfortunately, included amongst those ostensibly there to help were individuals who were tempted by the presence of unattended personal articles and valuables belonging to the dead and injured. As a result at 3.20 pm PC Powis found Matthew Fagan aged 43, a railway linesman based at Wembley station, acting suspiciously. Subsequently he was charged with larceny and in due course found guilty of stealing various items of cigarettes, food and clothing for which he was sent to prison for one month.

Such was the nature of the work that six police officers suffered slight injuries, necessitating in two cases their subsequently being placed on the sick list. There was also some damage to both police and civilian clothing, such as tears and blood stains and, perhaps more alarmingly, a three inch diameter burn hole from an oxy-acetylene torch in a mackintosh. Finally, as might be expected after such an extensive and prolonged operation, a certain amount of police equipment and personal property could not be located on conclusion of the operation, including two policeman's torches; a fire extinguisher; three blankets; two stretchers; a first aid kit; two waterproof sheets; overalls; six towels; a first aid kit; a fireman's axe; a hacksaw; an 18 inch Stiltson wrench; and a crowbar.

As usual with almost all incidents in which the police are involved, this accident was the subject of a written report, in this case of some length. When first received by senior officers, however, it was deemed to be inadequate and was rewritten to provide a basis for instruction during training. Copies were circulated to all Chief Superintendents and the Police College at Ryton-on-Dunsmore, Warwickshire.

Casualty Enquiry Offices

The small local police station 300 yards from the scene was rapidly overwhelmed as anxious relatives desperately sought news of family or friends believed to have been on the trains. Soon local people formed a queue outside the station, whilst others from all over the country telephoned for information. To deal with this, Mr A. Hoare, Manager of H.W. Perry Ltd, dealers in Ford motor cars at the Automobile Showrooms, The Bridge, Wealdstone agreed to the police using the premises as a temporary casualty enquiry office. This was set up at 9.40 am in the motor showroom and one small office. Two telephone lines were made available to Sergeant Cartwright and three constables under the direction of Inspector Salter, later augmented by a further two constables and a pair of women constables, seated at tables in the showroom. These dealt with a steady stream of concerned relatives, friends and employers seeking information on those who might have been on the train and sent messages to and from hospitals. By 10.30 am the volume of enquiries was such that it became necessary to set up a further team in Wealdstone police station itself to deal exclusively with business arising due to the accident, the normal staff there being supplemented by an inspector, a sergeant and eight constables. At the same time the number of telephone calls anticipated resulted in the GPO being requested to install additional temporary lines. By 12.45 pm one extra line permitted the transfer of a further two constables to Perry's showroom, while six further lines were installed at Wealdstone police station by 2.00 pm.

In view of the number of Her Majesty's Forces personnel involved in the accident, Major Jouning of the Registrar General's Staff, Royal Army Medical Corps at the Herbert Hospital, Woolwich was dispatched as liason officer to deal with any matters relating to them and he arrived at 4.40 pm. From then on he was able to assist in identification, locating military units, informing next of kin and taking custody of property. Later in the day as those people expected to return from work in the evening failed to do so, often merely because their journey home was severely disrupted by the blocked line, the rate of enquiries increased. The temporary office remained in use for two days, being closed and its work combined with that at Wealdstone from noon on Thursday 9th October. Police officers were on duty in every hospital involved from where progress reports with names and state of casualties were telephoned to headquarters at Wealdstone. As names became available and were confirmed, they were transmitted on to the Information Room at Scotland Yard in London, who then informed relatives by telegram, telephone or by means of provincial forces.

It was the job of the officers in these casualty enquiry offices to collate, in the days before computers, by hand, all available information on the casualties by instituting and cross checking suitably indexed registers of casualties notified and identified and of all persons about whom enquiries had been made from which lists of missing persons could be compiled. By this means they were able to undertake the often harrowing task of advising enquirers of the up-to-date position with regard to the dead, injured and unharmed. A large numbers of telephone calls were made, or messages passed to police stations throughout the country, to inform relatives and friends and in some cases request their attendance at hospitals to visit the seriously injured, or mortuaries to identify the dead. Communication between the two offices was maintained by a pair of police motorcycle dispatch riders, while the staff from the Press Bureau kept the press informed. A printed list of the casualties was prepared for distribution and subsequent amendments issued to all police stations to enable enquiries to be answered without delay.

By Saturday 11th October most of the outstanding missing persons had been accounted for, as many initially unaccounted for returned safely following a protracted journey home. By the next day, Sunday, three bodies remained unidentified and 15 persons continued to be missing, however, all the missing persons were tracked down by the Monday and only one body continued to be unidentified. This man had a ticket from Liverpool to Bournemouth and the assistance of the police forces in those two places was sought, fingerprints taken and descriptions published in the national press, initially without success. A touched up photograph was about to be circulated, when the Liverpool police provided information leading to his identification eight days after the accident, thus allowing the casualty enquiry office in Wealdstone police station to close.

One of the tasks of the casualty office was to compile figures for the numbers of dead, the injured detained in hospital or those treated but discharged, for inclusion in the several situation reports sent to the Information Room. This toll is indicated below:

The Advancing Toll of Casualties

Day & date October	Time	Dead in hospital	Detained	Treated in hospital but not detained
Wednesday 8th	10.28 am	6		40 to 50 injured
Thursday 9th	4.40 pm	90	91	63
Friday 10th	7.55 am	95	87	
	4.10 pm	105	87	
Saturday 11th	8.00 am	107	96	
	4.00 pm	108	96	
Tuesday 14th	12.20 pm	110	91	
Thursday 16th	7.55 am	112	91	

In addition, others who received minor injuries treated on site brought the total up to 399 casualties.

Assistance by Others and Visitors

By chance Harrow Council's Deputy Clerk had called a conference of Civil Defence officers to discuss organising 'work in an emergency' and delegates were just assembling, when they found they had a real one of some magnitude on their very doorstep and workers rushed to the scene with their equipment,

At night a member of the YMCA (Young Men's Christian Association) dispenses cups of tea to rescue workers. *Anthony V. Gregory*

arriving at 10.25 am. The assistance of Middlesex County Council Civil Defence Corps was requested at 11.30 am and nine men in a civil defence vehicle set off from Willesden at 2.30 pm. In due course some 50 to 60 Civil Defence workers, from the Harrow sub-division together with six from county headquarters at Wembley, were engaged in rescue operations for three days and nights with limited breaks. They spent the first day mostly recovering bodies. Their headquarters was set up in Carne's radio shop in Masons Avenue opposite the station. Stretchers and other equipment were obtained from their depot in Elmgrove Road, a short distance south of the station. Although the men tunnelled into the mass of wreckage, they were unable to reach some of the carriages of the local train or the locomotive of the Perth express train until the coaches burying them had been removed.

Others came to assist in both a practical and spiritual way. These included priests and ministers of several denominations; members of the Salvation Army; St John's Ambulance Brigade from Wembley; the Women's Voluntary Service; and YMCA. The British Red Cross contributed by sending Dr L.K. Wills, its Medical Officer and five nurses to Wembley Hospital and others to Central Middlesex and Harrow hospitals, while members of the Society were later involved in ferrying casualties home from hospitals, making 138 journeys. Major D. McAlonan of the Salvation Army, travelling in the guard's van of the local train, although initially shocked, soon waded in to help. In due course a number of rescue workers had to be ordered home due to exhaustion after working long hours.

Many offers of practical assistance were made by local residents, traders and engineering firms in the neighbourhood. Those who sent staff and lent equipment, included seven men from Rogers Coals of Harrow; 15 men from Kirk & Kirk of Wealdstone; three men from Ruddock & Meighan of Harrow View, Wealdstone, who stayed until 7.30 pm; and medical supplies were made available from the branch of Boots in the High Street. Various motor garages in the vicinity offered jacking and cutting equipment. Local housewives tore up sheets for bandages, while other local members of the community offered accommodation to the injured and relatives of those killed. Other organisations that provided help included Kodak Ltd, who sent their fire pump and four men led by Captain Anderson, together with nursing staff and refreshments; and British Oxygen Co. Ltd, who arrived at 9.50 am with oxy-acetylene cutters and operatives; while Cox & Danks Ltd, steel merchants, sent oxy-acetylene cutting equipment for use by the railway, which arrived at about 1.30pm

Parties of about 12 teenage boys from the Wealdstone and Harrow YMCA rendered assistance under the supervision of Mr H.E. Hepworth, General Secretary of the branch. They worked in shifts from early in the morning until midnight. Likewise the Salvation Army was on hand firstly manning the Kodak canteen and later, once their own canteen had arrived from headquarters, jointly running both with helpers from the Wealdstone and Harrow citadels under the charge of Senior Captain and Mrs W. Griggs. In addition Rover Scouts and Boy Scout troops offered their help, but were politely declined.

The welfare of the rescued and rescuers was arranged by Harrow Urban District Council, who called out the Harrow branch of the WVS on Wednesday morning. Their canteen, staffed continuously from 10.00 am until the end of rescue operations, by shifts of about eight women drawn from three local area branches provided tea and sandwiches under the supervision of Mrs Nixon, with many local trades people and residents offering gifts of tea, sugar, bread, etc. For the rescue teams, refreshment and wash rooms, supplied by kettles boiled in the station offices, were set up in some of the platform buildings. It is difficult nowadays for those of us used to 24 hour shopping, to realise how rigidly half-day closing was observed in those days; nonetheless some shops adjacent to the station stayed open that Wednesday afternoon to help with provisions. An impromptu canteen is reported as having been set up in the waiting room on Platform 1 at the instigation of over 20 local residents from Marlborough Road, Marlborough Hill, Marlborough Rise, Greenhill Road in Wealdstone, together with others from Stanmore, Mill Hill and Pinner. In the initial stages, all ingredients were provided by the volunteers, but owing to ongoing food rationing an approach was made to the Hotels Department of BR for further supplies, which were freely given.

Other people contacted the Police; Harrow UDC; Harrow Central Residents Association; and WVS to offer assistance, such as accommodation for the relatives of casualties wishing to visit the site and cars to transport them to the hospitals or mortuaries. Some advantage was taken of these kind offers, particularly of personal transport. These included members of the Harrow Round Table and the Harrow Rotary Club, together with the staff of Clarke & Co., auctioneers and estate agents and S.A. Sayce, house furnisher allowed their cars to be used to take relatives of casualties to hospital and mortuaries. During the ensuing days and weeks, council welfare officers visited the bereaved families.

The sudden increase in telephone traffic emanating from the Harrow area following the accident, as the authorities attempted to put in place their emergency plans and as passengers endeavoured to contact their places of work or relatives to say they were safe, together with the secondary traffic thereby generated, is reported to have overloaded the telephone system to the point where the dialling system actually broke down. As a consequence the 10 regular operators at Harrow exchange had to be supplemented by a further five to help deal manually with the traffic in calls. In addition to the temporary additional lines installed by the GPO to the Casualty Offices, a temporary telephone box was set up adjacent to the one existing public phone box at the station.

The availability of the good alternative transport facilities in the Harrow area, such as the Metropolitan at Harrow on the Hill with its connection on to Watford (Met) and the No. 142 bus route to the Stanmore branch of the Bakerloo line, as it then was – now the Jubilee line – meant there was no need for special arrangements for the uninjured passengers to continue their journey.

County councillors A.O. Loughlin and J.E. Odle paid visits to the site, together with the Chairman of the County Fire Brigade Committee to County Control and Vice-Chairman of the Fire Brigade Committee. The Rt Hon. A.T. Lennox-Boyd, the Minister of Transport, visited scene at 3.00 pm to see for himself how the rescue operations were proceeding.

Chapter Five

Personal Recollections

Mr and Mrs Nash's three daughters, aged thirteen, nine and five, having breakfasted after their father had already left for Watford Jn station to travel by train to work in London, attended school as usual on Wednesday 8th October and the younger two were in bed before he was due home. The next morning they went down to breakfast to find their mother Marjory in an awful state, having been awake all night waiting for her husband to return. Nonetheless, they went to school again, but during the lessons the middle daughter, Margaret, broke down crying to herself in class and was taken to the headmistress' sitting room to regain her composure. The following afternoon she and her youngest sister, Kate, were led in turn to the headmistress again, sat on her knee and with her arms around them, informed of their father's death in the accident, in response to which Margaret cried openly. That evening, once the younger two girls had settled in bed, their distraught mother came to them, but Margaret was afraid to show any emotion. As a consequence, without counselling and support for the family, such as Cruse Bereavement Care founded seven years later, her subsequent relationship with her mother deteriorated, becoming impersonal and with little mention of her father. For 10 years she felt very unhappy, leading to hospital treatment and a diagnosis of 'petit mal', rather than post-traumatic stress that we would recognise now, as she tried to come to terms with the loss. But in those days, there were few means of expressing one's feelings to draw out all the hurt and anguish that haunts her to this day.

In his early forties, William Kenneth Nash had been a senior clerk employed by the LMS, now with the Operating Department of London Midland Region, whose responsibilities included making arrangements for the running of the Royal train. Amongst his hobbies were railway photography and some of the results of this were published concurrently with the First Edition of this book in a book entitled *Cumbrian Railway Photographer*, compiled by his youngest daughter Kate Robinson. Compensation was offered to his dependants and in respect of the daughters initially amounting to £1,000, £600 and £400 each respectively, but how does one place a value on the loss of a father, who will not be there to share in listening to beautiful music, travelling, or just a normal happy family life? So, to represent their case, a lawyer was retained and the eventual recompense invested in 3¼% Funding Stock, but nothing would ever bring back their father.

Other schoolgirls were haunted by the knowledge, when going past the wreckage, that some of their friends on one of the trains involved would never be at school again. Even years later, a remainder of the event could bring distress back again necessitating counselling all those years on.

David Dean was a 22-year-old trainee civil engineer travelling up from his parents' home at Hemel Hempstead to his place of work in the Chief Civil Engineer's Works Office at Euston station in the last coach of the local train. Not only was his left leg trapped by the tangled wreckage, but hydrochloric acid was trickling down on his forehead from the lighting battery cells of the vehicle above him. Once he realised the latter problem, he was able to move a hand to deflect the drips. After some hours, he was found by Sidney Blackford, a 33-year-old general dealer of Harrow, who had managed to worm his way into the wreckage. Nonetheless, recovering Dean was a protracted process and for over two hours Blackford kept his mind occupied by chatting to him about football and general matters, while other rescuers worked away by hand to clear a way in. During this period Blackford, under the instructions of a doctor close by, administered a morphine injection and bandaged the injured foot. Dean was finally released at 1.20 pm and is believed to have been one of the last persons abstracted alive.

As the nearer hospitals were by then already full, he was taken by ambulance to the Central Middlesex Hospital at Park Royal, Harlesden, where he was to stay for three months. Here he was attended to by the orthopaedic surgeon, Mr Bonning, who was able to save the knee, which so greatly aided Dean's future mobility, that, once recovery was complete, many were unaware of his disability. Indeed after 21 months, including a skin graft at the West Middlesex Hospital to repair the damage caused by the acid, he was able to resume work and in due course carry out all the usual duties of a railway civil engineer, including full access to the track and climbing ladders to carry out bridge inspections. The fact that he was able to achieve this, especially in the days before trauma counselling, was not of course without its heart aches. When he first realised that he had lost his leg, he was concerned that his girlfriend might no longer find him attractive, but with her support and that of his parents, together with his faith and the prayers of his fellow Christadelphians, as a young man he made a remarkable recovery. Three years later he married Patricia, his girlfriend, and they subsequently brought up three boys, two of whom work in the rail industry.

Arthur Collyer of Watford, a competitor in the 800 metres at the Berlin Olympics 1936 and, but for the war, was due to have been again in Finland in 1940, was employed in the General Manager's Office of the London Midland Region at Euston. He regularly travelled in the eighth coach of the local train from Watford and that day was on his way to Carlisle for a staff consultation meeting. He distinctly remembers, as his train pulled out of Harrow station, the engine of the Perth train hitting it, followed by the escaping steam, a horrendous noise and dust as his coach was overturned, after which he lost consciousness. He came to, perhaps a quarter of an hour later, when a rescuer trod on a plank resting on his leg. There had been 14 people in his compartment, now reduced to three feet in width, and he was extremely fortunate to emerge alive and largely unscathed. His coach ended up over the smokebox of the Perth engine No. 46242, causing his trousers to be blackened by smoke. After his discovery by rescuers and release from the remains of his compartment through a hole, he sat down in the sunshine to recover gradually, when he saw a friend, Mr Weald, unable to move due to his legs being broken. He later wandered around on the platform in a dazed and shocked state, but so soon after the accident all the fit and able were desperately searching for further injured amongst the wreckage. So, as there was apparently no one to attend to him, he took a No. 158 bus to Watford and walked to the Watford Peace Memorial Hospital, where at 10.00 am he reported to the hospital for attention to splinters of glass in his eye. There, at that time, they knew nothing of a major accident only six miles away. Afterwards, he boarded a bus home, where he was met by his wife who had just received a telephone message to say he had been seriously injured.

The London Midland Region hierarchy at Euston House had an arrangement to take the chill out of food rationing which, although much reduced by the time, was still in existence in the latter part of 1952. Once a week the Dublin office would make up a hamper of everything that could not be purchased in England and ship it over on the mail boat to Holyhead where it would be met by a Euston House messenger. Something went wrong on October 7th/8th and instead of returning on the Mail, the messenger changed at Crewe and travelled in the leading compartment of the up Perth. Although he survived, he was so traumatised that, despite spending 10 years in and out of hospital, 25 years later still used to wake up screaming in the middle of the night because he could hear the down Liverpool train whistling before it ran into the wreckage.

Sapper Maurice Leaky was one of only two soldiers out of a party of 10 or 12 travelling from Elgin on the Perth train to survive. Upon arrival at his unit of the British Army of the Rhine in Germany, the resulting trauma led to his being placed for some time on light duties in the armoury.

Just prior to the accident Arthur Ernest Arnold of Wealdstone, Manager for 47 years of Wyman's bookstall on platform Nos. 2 and 3 went onto the platform to retrieve a paper which had blown away towards the passenger footbridge. He noticed the 8.11 am local train, particularly crowded due to the cancellation of the subsequent 8.27 am train, and stood dumbfounded as the Perth train ploughed into its rear sending wreckage spewing towards him, immediately to be followed by the down express crashing into the obstruction. He had been within a yard of the platform edge and debris fell all around him, yet miraculously he remained untouched. After seeing the injured escape from the train, he was led home in a state of shock. Nonetheless, he had recovered sufficiently the next day and the following Saturday to be able to recount his experiences on BBC television.

Jack Foxley, a railway employee at the District Engineer's Office at St Pancras, formerly at Watford Jn, was lucky to escape from the fifth coach of the local train, which had been tilted sideways. The compartment had been full with at least four people standing, which made escape difficult. Upon extracting himself miraculously unhurt, he thought, having previously been involved in clearing up and reinstatement following some six or seven major accidents between Euston and Rugby, that he ought to make a record of the devastation, but in his dazed state was unable to concentrate. He was thereupon sent home and was off work for some days having been medically diagnosed as suffering from shock. Upon his return to work he was deliberately kept away from the essential clearing up work and restoration of the track and footbridge, etc. Nonetheless, he became conscious of the loss of friends. For instance, soon after he happened to visit the London Midland Region's Permanent Way Drawing Office at Euston and there found only three people at their desks, the remaining drawing boards of the dead and injured still with dust covers on.

At the beginning of World War II, Reg had volunteered for the RAF and, despite serving as a navigator on bombing raids, thereby escaped the fate of many of his fellow railway colleagues following their capture at Singapore, and survived the war. On resuming work with the railways and living in Watford, he travelled daily at the rear of the 7.31 am local train from Tring to Euston. It was just one of those things, that on the day of the accident, he had been sent to Nottingham to carry out an audit of a depot canteen accounts, yet again avoiding the tragic consequences of so many of his travelling colleagues.

Ron Meeking, as an assistant resident engineer in the Direct Labour Organisation of the LMR, was employed at the time on the construction of the carriage washing plant at Stonebridge Park, when mid-morning on 8th October he received an urgent instruction by telephone from the Operating Superintendent for the travelling crane and driver he was using to be sent with all haste to Harrow. This request was complied with resulting in drastic rearrangement of the work programme and led during the afternoon to Mr McIlmoyle, the New Works Engineer, demanding to know who had authorised the removal of the crane without reference to him. On learning of the nature of the disaster at Harrow & Wealdstone, however, he had to eat humble pie. Likewise, Alec Swain, who was an apprentice at the former North London Railway's works at Bow, East London, recalls the arrival of a lorry to undertake the urgent requisitioning of oxy-acetylene cutting gear, as much more than the normal allocation of a breakdown train was needed.

The 7.31 am from Tring was Henry Casserley's regular train to work in London. This usually consisted of a nine-coach train made up of a standard Euston to Watford seven non-corridor coach set with two 'swingers' at the rear as strengtheners. As the holder of a railway photographic lineside permit and well known to the station staff, he was in the habit of walking from his house adjoining the line through the goods yard at Berkhampstead to the north end of platform 4 to join the back of the train. These coaches at the rear were usually emptier and were often of pre-Grouping origin and, if ex-LNWR vehicles, more comfortable than LMS standard stock. Perhaps luckily for him in the long run, because there were very few survivors from the last two coaches, he was taken ill with bronchitis on Friday 3rd October and was off work for a week. He made a trip up the line to see the smash on Friday 10th October and only returned to work the next day, after which many familiar faces were missing from his fellow commuters.

Mr C.W. Herbert on the other hand, lived on the west side of the line just outside Harrow & Wealdstone station and he was in the habit of catching the 8.15 am Bakerloo tube train to reach London. Having boarded this train on 8th October, it set off as usual, only to come to an abrupt halt unaware that a double collision had occurred just behind them and the leading engines of the Liverpool train had short-circuited the traction current. Moments earlier he might have been still standing on the platform at risk from the flying debris. Instead, after a while, the passengers were led along the track to Kenton station. Included amongst these was Audrey Austin of Carmelite Road, backing on to the railway between Headstone Lane and Harrow & Wealdstone, travelling to work in the City in the last coach. On hearing the crash, her father went to the allotments adjacent to the line and saw the steam and dust rising from the scene of the accident. He then set off for the station and was unable to find his daughter, but fortunately she was able to telephone through to home to say she was safe.

Likewise passengers in the following southbound tube train, which was stopped short of the station, were disembarked and had to cross people's gardens and pass through their houses to reach safety. Included amongst these were the wife and six-year-old son of police constable Krafft on their way from their home in Hatch End to Neasden. PC 158X Don Krafft himself, although stationed at Wealdstone police station, was on late turn, but on hearing of the crash on the radio cycled into work. Here he was allocated to the Casualty Bureau set up in the motor show room and was one of those on the hectic task of handling the numerous enquiries, while his personal concerns for his wife and son had to take second place until he managed to get a short break. Then contact with his son's school revealed that he had not yet arrived and only later did they ring back to say he had turned up safely. Later he moved back to the police station and helped to compile the casualty list.

On the morning in question police constable Mick Walker was just washing down his motorcycle, one of the first equipped with radio, before breakfast during his early turn (6.00 am to 2.00 pm), when the garage sergeant sent him down to Harrow & Wealdstone station. His bike was therefore the first vehicle there with a radio, so he acted as a control until another radio vehicle arrived. Likewise PC 574X Richard Dickinson of Wembley Police Garage was on traffic patrol duty in the Harrow area, when, just after 8.00 am, the call came to proceed urgently to the railway station. He believes his was the second vehicle on the scene of what was certainly one of the worst incidents in his career. Both of them and their colleagues worked on rescue and recovery work for the rest of that day and eventually signed off at about 9.00 or 10.00 pm. The whole incident was comprehensively recorded by hand in the Occurrence Book at Wealdstone police station by Sub Divisional Inspector Ivan Bray. The emergency services did not possess the quality of equipment which prevails today and Dickinson can recall the police 'requisitioning' some the tools necessary for rescue work from a local hardware shop.

Following breakfast, young PC 362X Ken Rowland of Uxbridge was sent with others to Harrow to assist the police at that station. Once on the scene, he was detailed to relieve a fellow badly in need of a break and joined a team on search and rescue duties under the direction of an inspector. The wreckage was systematically searched, but by this time only in the forlorn hope of finding anyone still alive. The bodies and limbs recovered were removed by ambulance to the temporary mortuary and where Rowland was in due course to continue his duties.

Probationer police constable 487X Ken Lemming of Wealdstone police station had completed his turn of night duty on the beat and was sound asleep in his home a quarter of a mile north of the station. He was aware that something shook the house, but it was not until around 10.00 am that another policeman called and summoned him, along with many more like him, back on duty. Like PC Rowland, he was sent with others to assist the keeper of the mortuary half a mile away in making lists of the fatal casualties and property brought in from the site. Under the direction of a senior officer, their task was to write an identification number on luggage labels and attach them to the recovered bodies and severed parts. In addition they removed clothing in an effort to identify the person concerned; a very harrowing experience, not for the faint hearted. In the evening they were relieved. Lemming returned the next morning and later was transferred to a team sorting out personal property and valuables recovered from the site.

John Moss attended from the second day as the recently promoted Deputy Superintendent Ambulance Officer and learnt a lot. He and his colleagues became aware that their service had been ill-prepared to cope with an accident on such a huge scale. They realised that, whilst all the emergency services had worked hard, many to the point of exhaustion, improvisation had been the order of the day. There remained inter-service rivalry and there had been no overall co-ordinated plan on how to handle such a situation. By the early evening of the second day, only 85 of the 112 casualties had been recovered and it was the early hours of the fourth day before the last body was retrieved. As a consequence of his recognition of his own inexperience at Harrow, he started to take an interest in planning for major emergencies, an area of work he was to pursue for the rest of his career, ending up as Chief Operational Officer of the London Ambulance Service.

Mrs D. West had served as a woman police constable during World War II, but by 1952 had married and settled down to bring up two children in flat above the grocer's Cullens in Wealdstone High Street. On hearing the noise of the first crash, she went to the station to offer assistance, but was asked to return in an hour, which she did. As well as making way for stretchers being carried out of a side door, she recalls Revd H.E. Stewart, the Vicar of Holy Trinity Church sitting beside others badly wounded and singing a hymn. Having helped by moving some debris from the track and platform to stack against the retaining wall, she assisted by tearing up sheets to make bandages and, after being interviewed by a newspaper reporter, left the scene exhausted after four hours. A few days later she listened to the memorial service at Holy Trinity Church relayed by loud speaker. For long afterwards the distressing memory of the crash haunted her and prevented her travelling by train for some six months.

Michael Cobb grew up and lived in the locality for 30 years. As a small boy he used to stand by the little gate on the east side, waiting for his father to return from work. He would watch the Stanmore motor train come and go, together with a 0-6-2T wheeze its way north on the Broad Street trains, which often had great difficulty starting away from the station. In due course, he joined the Royal Engineers and became a surveyor, yet retained his enthusiasm for the railways. In 1952 he was living in Harrow on the Hill, from where he drove to work at the Ordnance Survey in Chessington. On the morning of 8th October he could not think what all the ambulances were doing that kept passing him, until his wife informed of the accident on his return that evening. He was filled with horror, realising that he frequently caught the steam instead of the electric train from Harrow to London and always found a seat in the last compartment, as it was usually empty. His wife was one of those with a car who volunteered to ferry passengers around and she took an American off the Liverpool train back to London. Her passenger had been slightly injured in the arm as a result of being thrown through the window on the rebound from the initial impact and sliding across the platform on his backside.

Major Cobb knew one of the doctors who lived in Kenton who had been helping to deal with the injured and between them they contrived for Cobb to don a white coat and go along as the doctor's assistant. An evening or so later they entered through the booking office around 9.00 pm and on to platform 4 to stand by the *City of Glasgow* and see the pitiful site of the crushed cab, concluding that, while awful, the enginemen's deaths must at least have been quick.

The dust of the accident had barely settled when Peter Brannan from Harrow View, a reporter for the *Harrow Observer*, arrived on the scene at about 8.40 am on his bicycle, as people were still stumbling about. He reports the ground fog was still quite thick although likely to be burnt off by the sun quite quickly. Within about 10 minutes, aware of the enormity of the disaster and as local correspondent for Reuters and the Press Association, he phoned his contacts in Fleet Street from the Newsagent in Marlborough Hill and received £20 for his troubles. He told them that there must be at least 100 dead and that they should, 'Get somebody out here'. Without exception he was told to 'Pull himself together', but he was not far out, as we know, the final toll being 112 dead and many hundreds more injured.

The disaster occurred on the weekly *Observer's* press day, and he should have been on his way to Uxbridge with his Editor to help put the paper together, but he phoned in with the news of the crash and was told to stay there to get as much information as he could. Tony 'Greg' Gregory an amateur freelance photographer and friend, who regularly provided material and lived about 150 yards from the station, was already on the scene when Brannan arrived. Together they spent almost as much time helping people out of the wreckage as they did gathering news and pictures. The double collision had pushed the wreckage up under the covered passenger footbridge and they were able to help people climb up out of the wrecked carriages onto the remains of the footbridge. As the fog and steam cleared, the full extent of the disaster became apparent. The two locomotives of the northbound express that had ploughed through the wreckage of the Perth and local commuter trains, lay on their sides steaming and he was wary of getting too close to them for fear of explosion.

When Brannan finally arrived in Uxbridge, having phoned his story ahead, he found that a couple of very poor pictures from another freelance photographer had been plated and were ready for press. He told his Editor that Greg had very much better pictures, but the response was that there was not time to muck about; they had to go to press. Fortunately the Editor-in-Chief overheard his protestations and insisted on driving him back to Harrow to see Greg and get prints of some of his photographs. As a result the front page was remade using three of Greg's excellent shots for which he received the standard *Observer* fee of one guinea each! The undeveloped films of other pictures were sent direct to press agencies in London and some used in the national papers. The time he spent away from his regular job at the Ministry of Food, led to Greg losing his job and launched him on a full time career as a professional press photographer.

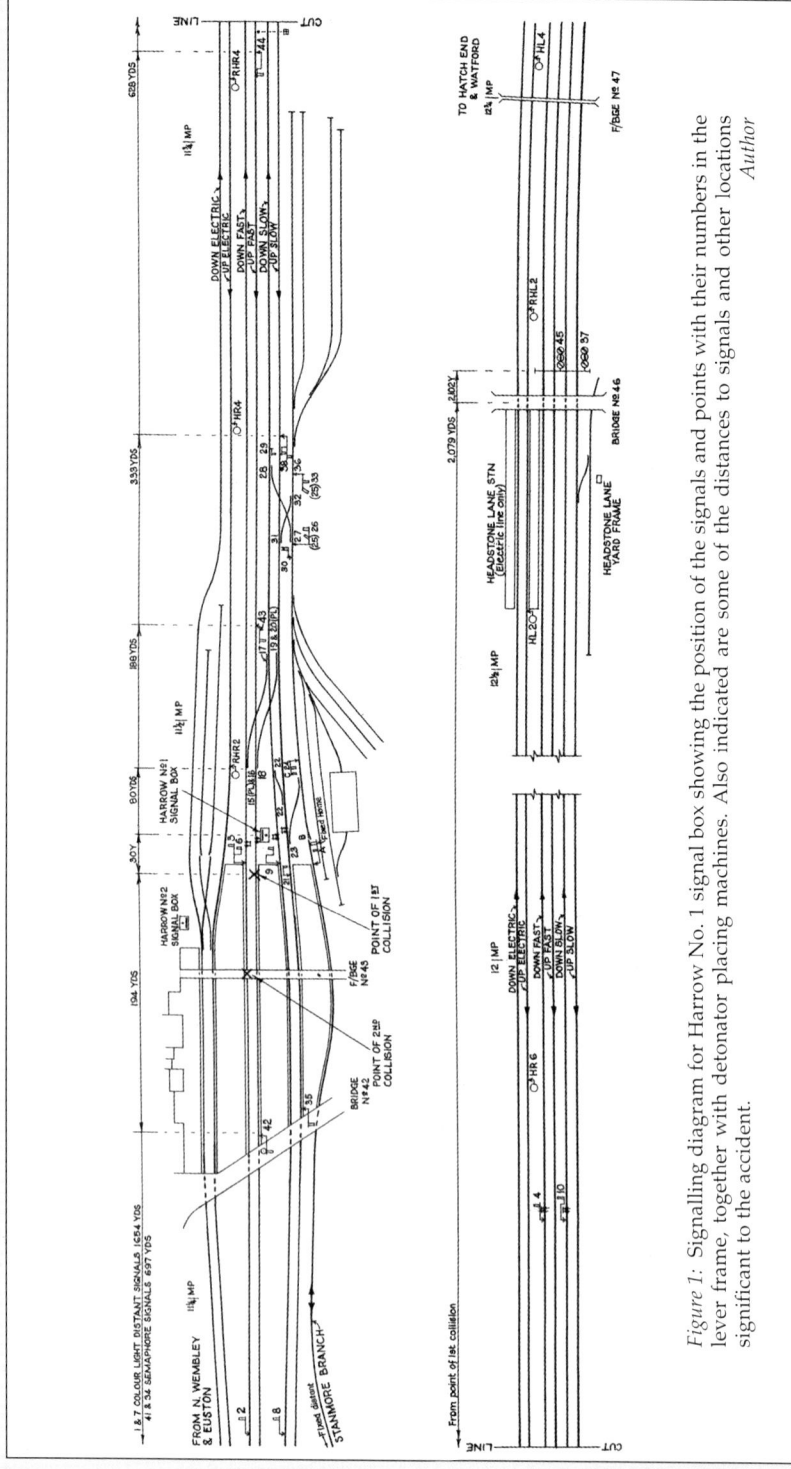

Figure 1: Signalling diagram for Harrow No. 1 signal box showing the position of the signals and points with their numbers in the lever frame, together with detonator placing machines. Also indicated are some of the distances to signals and other locations significant to the accident.

Author

Chapter Six

Clearing the Wreckage

On the occasion of any major accident, one of the first people summoned to the site is the District Engineer (DE) for the locality. By 1952 such officers were provided with an official car and in view of the likely disruption to ordinary rail services, this would be the preferred means of reaching the site of such an incident. Having inspected the scene and taken stock of the situation, one of his first tasks is likely to be, and always in the case of a fatality, to arrange for a survey of the site to be made before too much of the evidence is disturbed by the efforts to clear the line for use first at the internal inquiry and subsequently at the Ministry of Transport (MOT) inquiry. The DE in this case was based on two floors of the former hotel at St Pancras station, where he had about a dozen technical staff, together with clerical staff and two chief inspectors, one for permanent way and the other for works, each with a small number of staff. To undertake the survey it would be necessary to locate at short notice one or two of his technical staff, who would be assisted by a chainman. The resulting drawing would probably be based on the existing survey, often at 40 feet to 1 inch scale, usually available for all stations with all the existing details marked in. The survey of the scene of the accident, copied from the Inspector's report, following the double collision at Harrow and Wealdstone is the basis of *Figure 2* reproduced overleaf.

In the days of small gangs of men each with their length of track to look after, the local permanent way staff would be on site almost immediately. A.H. Payne, the ganger will have immediately summoned C.E. Penny, the permanent way inspector, in this case based at Watford. The availability of other gangs up and down the line would provide the source of considerable manpower to assist in clearing the line. As it was to turn out, this accident was to take nearly five days to clear and men from further afield would be brought in on a shift basis to enable the men initially on site to take a well earned rest.

Where the track was damaged, it would be the DE's responsibility to have this repaired before the lines could be re-opened. In this case several lengths of plain line would have to be relaid, whilst replacement switches and crossings would have had to be obtained from the Central Materials Depot at Northampton, or even specially made in a hurry, to enable the double slip in the up electric line at the entrance to the berthing siding to be restored.

Generally, the relief work was carried through in a quiet efficient manner, under the difficult conditions imposed by the magnitude and complexity of the wreckage and the constriction of the site. Many well deserved public tributes have been paid to all who were concerned with this task. Travelling on the local train were a number of senior railway officials. These included Mr S. Williams, the S&T Engineer, and Mr F.W. Abraham, the Motive Power Superintendent, who promptly advised railway headquarters and remained on site to assist in co-ordinating rescue and recovery work. So it was that the smooth working of the arrangements as a whole was due in no small measure to the general direction of Mr S.G. Hearn, Operating Superintendent, London Midland Region, who, following his arrival at

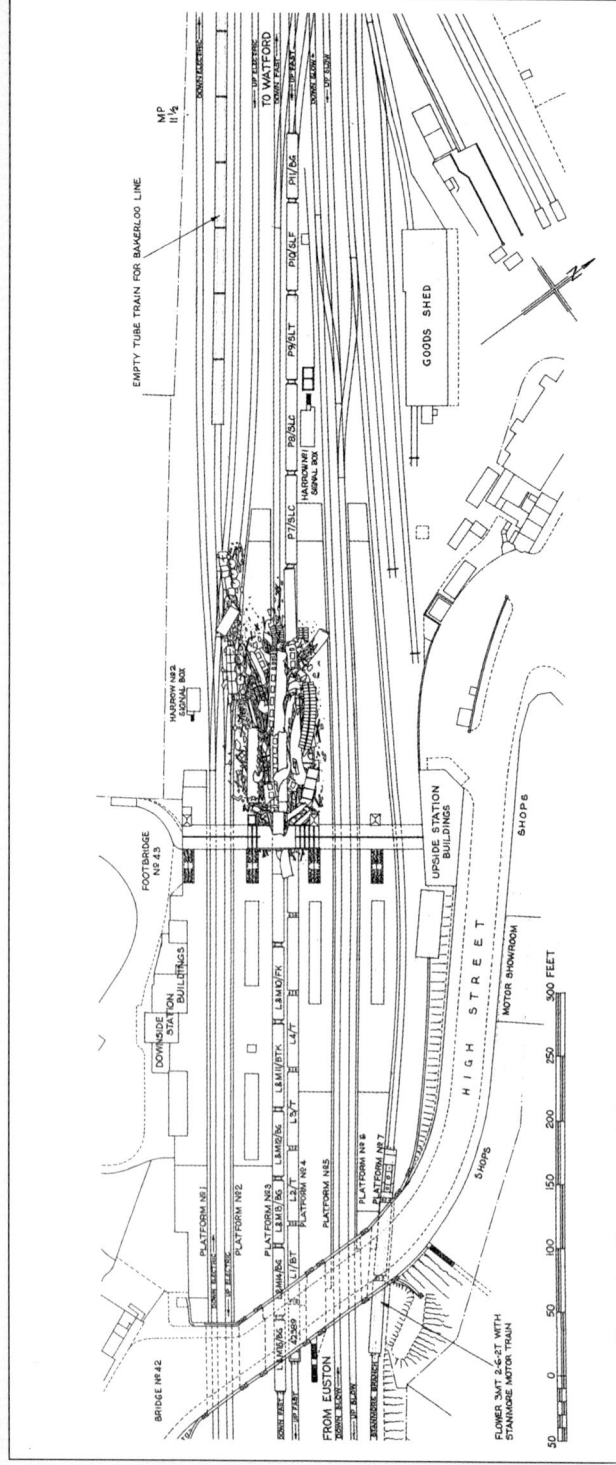

Figure 2: The scene of chaos immediately following the double collision at Harrow and Wealdstone station at 8.18 am on 8th October, 1952, when the 8.15 pm overnight sleeping car train from Perth to Euston ran into the rear of the 7.31 am outer suburban train from Tring to Euston. This was followed almost immediately by the double-headed 8.00 am express train from Euston to Liverpool and Manchester and as the motor train from Belmont was about to arrive. The momentum of the two locomotives of the Liverpool and Manchester train projected them onto the electric lines just after a London-bound train had left.   *Author*

9.05 am, set up a railway control point in a room on platform 6. It was Mr Williams who organised temporary GPO and railway telephone services, the latter connected to Euston, Crewe and Watford, and Mr Abraham, who took immediate steps to summon heavy steam cranes to the site and then remained without a break to direct the work of the breakdown gangs until at least the next morning. In due course he worked in conjunction with the District Operating Superintendent, Mr L.W. Cox, who was in immediate charge of the operating side of the work. By about 11.00 am, with most of the casualties removed, the railway authorities took over responsibility for the remaining rescue and recovery operations, although the Metropolitan Police maintained control outside the station. Early in the afternoon LMS 4-4-0 '2P' No. 40659 is reported to have arrived with an officer's saloon from Crewe. By evening flood lighting had been set up to enable work to continue through the night, but this was hampered when by 7.00 pm fog returned.

The blockage of this main route to the North was in effect total. For although the up and down slow lines were obstructed by only light debris, a temporary walkway had to be maintained across them for some time to enable the casualties to be evacuated to the ambulances in the goods yard on the east side. Later these two lines were obstructed by one of the breakdown cranes working to clear the debris. It is understood that the first breakdown gang on site was from London Transport, who are thought to have arrived by motor vehicle. The MOT and police reports indicate that the 30 ton crane from Willesden arrived at 9.40 am and was manoeuvred into position on the down electric line by 10.45 am and this was followed at 11.28 am by the 50 ton crane from Rugby which was in position by 1.25 pm on the up slow line. However, the author's studies of breakdown cranes and in particular their allocation suggest that the location of these two cranes was transposed. At the time the crane at Willesden was No. RS1015/50, one of a pair of Craven Bros cranes built in 1931 as a 36 ton crane and strengthened in 1938/9 to a maximum capacity of 50 tons, whereas the crane allocated to Rugby was No. RS1075/30, a 30 ton crane built by Cowans Sheldon in 1943 (*see below*). Willesden was nearer, and its breakdown train arrived on site first, having had to gain access to the electric lines and pass one presumes a larger number of LMR electric and London Underground trains likewise at a standstill until released. It would also have had to be shunted to place the crane ahead of the engine. The Rugby train, on the other hand, had the

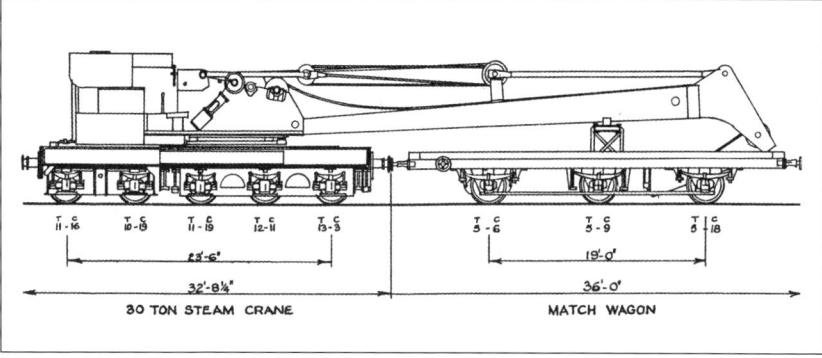

Diagram of LMS 30 ton Cowans Sheldon steam breakdown crane of the type allocated to Rugby in 1952. *Author*

benefit of the alternative route via Northampton and quadruple track from there by which to circumnavigate the inevitable congestion of passenger and freight trains delayed by the blockage of the line. The aerial photographs taken by Aerofilms during the early afternoon of 8th October, show the 30 ton crane already at work and RS1015/50 apparently only preparing to start work. They were followed by the Cowans Sheldon 36 ton crane from Kentish Town No. RS1008/36, which had arrived at 12.40 pm and was brought into use at 3.35 pm. Later the crane from Crewe arrived at 9.55 pm. This was one of three Cowans Sheldon cranes also built as a 36 ton crane in 1931 and like the Craven cranes strengthened to 50 ton capacity in 1938/9. The Kentish Town crane having developed a defect, the Ransomes & Rapier 45 ton crane No. 16 of 1940 from Old Oak Common, Western Region was brought in as a replacement, leaving shed at 12.25 pm and arriving at 3.45 pm on the following day, 9th October.

Steam Breakdown Cranes Used to Clear Wreckage

No.	Region	Depot	Builder	Year	Max. capacity tons	@ radius ft	Wheel arrmt
RS1015/50	LMR	Willesden	Craven Bros	1931	50	18	4-8-4RB
RS1075/30	LMR	Rugby	Cowans Sheldon	1943	30	16	0-6-4
RS1008/36	LMR	Kentish Town	Cowans Sheldon	1917	36	23	4-6-0
RS1005/50	LMR	Crewe North	Cowans Sheldon	1931	50	18	4-8-4RB
16	WR	Old Oak Common	Ransomes & Rapier	1940	45	20	4-8-4RB

Notes:
1. The wheel arrangement is expressed in Whyte's notation with the crane considered as normally leading with the jib in train formation. RB indicates that detachable relieving bogies are fitted.
2. Maximum capacity quoted for crane in propped condition with propping girders extended and either jacks screwed down where fitted, or girders well wedged up, on a substantial bed of timber packing.

The protracted task of clearing the wreckage was carried through with determination by men from the Motive Power Department's breakdown gangs, Engineer's and Signal & Telegraph departments with some assistance from the Operating Department, who worked untiringly with the minimum of rest and relief until late on Saturday, 11th October. In the days of steam operation and largely hand maintenance of the track, large resources of manpower could be summoned to undertake the work. The force of the double impact meant that the colliding vehicles were forced together, resulting in much distortion and telescoping, making the task of lifting and setting pieces down clear of the track much more difficult. Large breakdown cranes are relatively unstable and their use calls for considerable experience and great care, particularly by the supervisor and the driver. They have been known to turn over and this is not only bad news for the crane and its driver, but those who necessarily may be standing close by. A crane's maximum capacity is only available at minimum radius and when propped by a number of transverse telescopic beams in the crane carriage which must be drawn out and supported by being jacked down onto, or wedged up off, timber packing to distribute the propping force onto the underlying ground. This means the crane cannot move along the track in this condition and once 'free on rail' to enable it to make a move at slow speed along the track, the lifting capacity is reduced to approximately one-third. In either condition, as the radius increases the permitted load reduces quite markedly to less than half at maximum radius. To reach out over the wreckage the cranes were often working at full load, or more, and it is therefore of paramount importance that the lift should be made cleanly and continuously without snagging on adjacent wreckage.

Breakdown gangs are usually manned by resident staff from the depot to which the crane is allocated with just the driver permanently allotted the task of looking after the crane full time and keeping it in light steam. Thus the shed master or mechanical foremen would be in charge of operations and the gang would be made up of fitters, boilermakers and labourers summoned from their everyday tasks. In those days being a member of the breakdown gang had its attractions, as a means of obtaining extra overtime. This system worked well enough for all the usual incidents which seldom took more than 24 hours to clear up.

As part of the review of activities and reorganisation of the Motive Power Department, the LMS overhauled its arrangements for breakdown trains shortly before World War II. Each Motive Power District had its fully equipped breakdown train and crane, which by the mid-1940s was steam powered, usually allocated to the district headquarters, but occasionally to another main depot. Elsewhere in the district there might be one or two tool vans available to tackle smaller local incidents. The diagram to illustrate the form of a typical breakdown train showed a 0-6-0 '4F' tender locomotive, followed by a 30 ton steam crane, a three-plank drop-side wagon loaded with timber packing, a bogie tool van and a bogie mess/riding van. On such an occasion of course, any suitable locomotive to hand would be coupled up to the train, together where available, with the crane of whatever type allocated to that depot. Of the other vehicles in the train, it was soon found that open wagons allowed rainfall to permeate the timber packing and rot set in, so covered vans or sheeted wagons were preferred. The tool and mess vans were converted from redundant bogie coaching stock. The former was fitted out to accommodate the wide range of tools, including re-railing ramps; lifting tackle; jacks; hauling gear; cutting and lighting equipment, which experience suggested were necessary for breakdown work. The mess van was equipped to provide the breakdown gang with refreshment and respite for which it was fitted with cooking and drying facilities.

Initially the breakdown crew had to proceed with extreme caution and there was some delay to the lifting operations, due to the need to exercise great care until the search for the injured and the recovery and identification of the bodies had been completed. Instead much small debris was removed piece by piece by hand along a chain of men across the station. Baggage and personal belongings were diverted to a separate area for identification and, where possible, return to the owner or their next of kin. The five forward undamaged coaches of the local train were hauled away to Sudbury Jn to enable cranes to approach nearer to the wreckage, followed at 10.40 am by the rear five of the Perth train to Watford, together with four the rear of the Liverpool train at 4.15 pm to Sudbury Jn. The priority was to clear the slow lines and reopen at least a restricted service to Euston again. To this end crane No. RS1075/30 on the up slow started to clear smaller items of debris, but including a section of the roof to one of the carriages, and placing them on the Stanmore branch line (*see Figure 4*). Soon

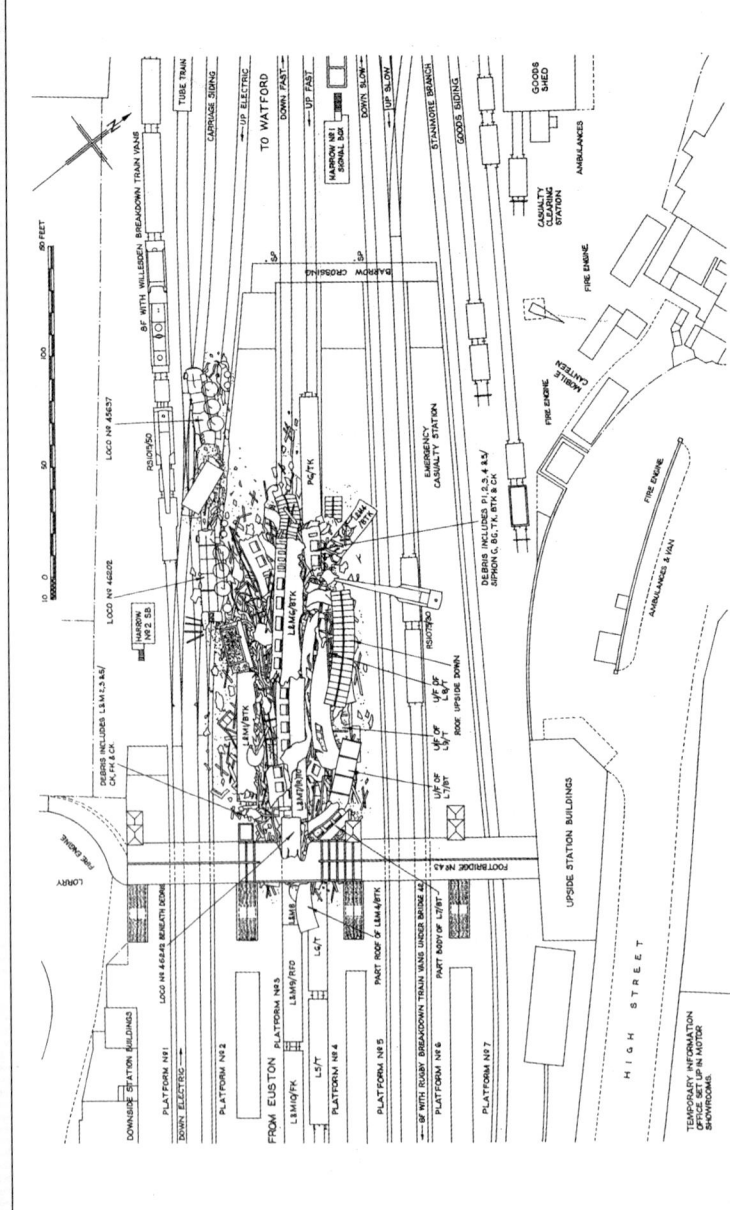

Figure 3: By the early afternoon of the same day, most of the undamaged coaches had been removed, but all lines are still blocked as the recovery of the dead and injured continues with two steam breakdown cranes already at work. An emergency casualty station was set up on the country end of platforms 6 and 7 and staffed by the United States Air Force medical teams.
Author

after 5.00 pm a train of empty bolster and plate wagons was placed on the down slow line to enable the crane to load these with debris. Shortly after 6.30 pm floodlights were switched on and from the evening of 8th October it became possible to work the cranes end on to the wreckage from the fast lines, whilst the up and down slow lines, which were largely undamaged, were reopened to traffic the next day, 9th October, at 5.32 am and 5.55 am respectively with a 5 mph speed restriction past the scene of the accident. The complete interruption of the West Coast main line route from Euston to the North had thus lasted for 21¼ hours. The first train through at 6.00 am was the 5.40 pm from Glasgow to Euston, which should have passed at 5.05 am.

In the meantime, the leading engine of the Manchester train, No. 45637 *Windward Islands* had been re-railed by cranes RS1015/50 and RS1008/36 standing on the down electric line and removed during the night of the 8th/9th October to the one of the electric carriage berthing sidings, this being one of a pair of tracks used by electric trains terminating at the station, the one nearest the main line being commandeered for the wrecked engines. Various other sundry pieces of wreckage from the engines were dumped alongside. The kitchen car to the Liverpool train, which had ridden up over the wreckage to a height level with the footbridge, was dragged away from the entangled wreckage by a hawser attached to a Stanier 2-8-0 class '8F' locomotive at 5.00 pm. No. 46202 *Princess Anne* was first restored to the upright position again by RS1015/50 and RS1008/36 (*see Figure 4 overleaf*). In attempting to lift its share of No. 46202, however, it seems probable that crane No. RS1008/36 was strained and as a consequence it had to retire for repairs. In its stead the Western Region's Ransomes and Rapier 45 ton crane No. 16 from Old Oak Common was called in, arriving at 3.45 pm via Acton Wells and Willesden. The second engine of this train was not, therefore, disposed of until 2.15 am on Friday, 10th October, when it too was placed in the siding. The remains of two coaches of the Liverpool train were lifted off the top of the last vehicles of the local train by 5.10 am. After which the Stanmore branch was cleared of debris by 7.00 am and utilised for stabling of vehicles waiting to be loaded, until 8.00 pm the next day. Even then the electric lines still could not be released for some time. Initially they were occupied by the cranes working on the coaches and disposing of the debris, which cleared at 3.55 am on 11th October, permitting the points to be clipped for the straight run through. This allowed the Old Oak Common crane to be released to return to shed at 4.04 am on 11th October. The electric lines were not therefore reopened to traffic until 4.30 am, after which the 1 in 7½ double slip connection complete except for the outside crossing will have had to be renewed. Work of this nature means risk to those involved in clearing the line and in this case three rescue workers were badly injured during the first night and taken to hospital themselves. Several others received minor injuries from falling wreckage, but were treated at the first-aid posts on the station.

Until the mass of wreckage, under which the engine of the Perth train lay buried, had been removed and the damaged girders of the footbridge cut away, No. 46242 *City of Glasgow* could not be recovered from the down fast line. It was finally uncovered on Saturday 11th October, re-railed by 10.10 am and drawn clear at 12 noon. This allowed the permanent way to be temporarily repaired,

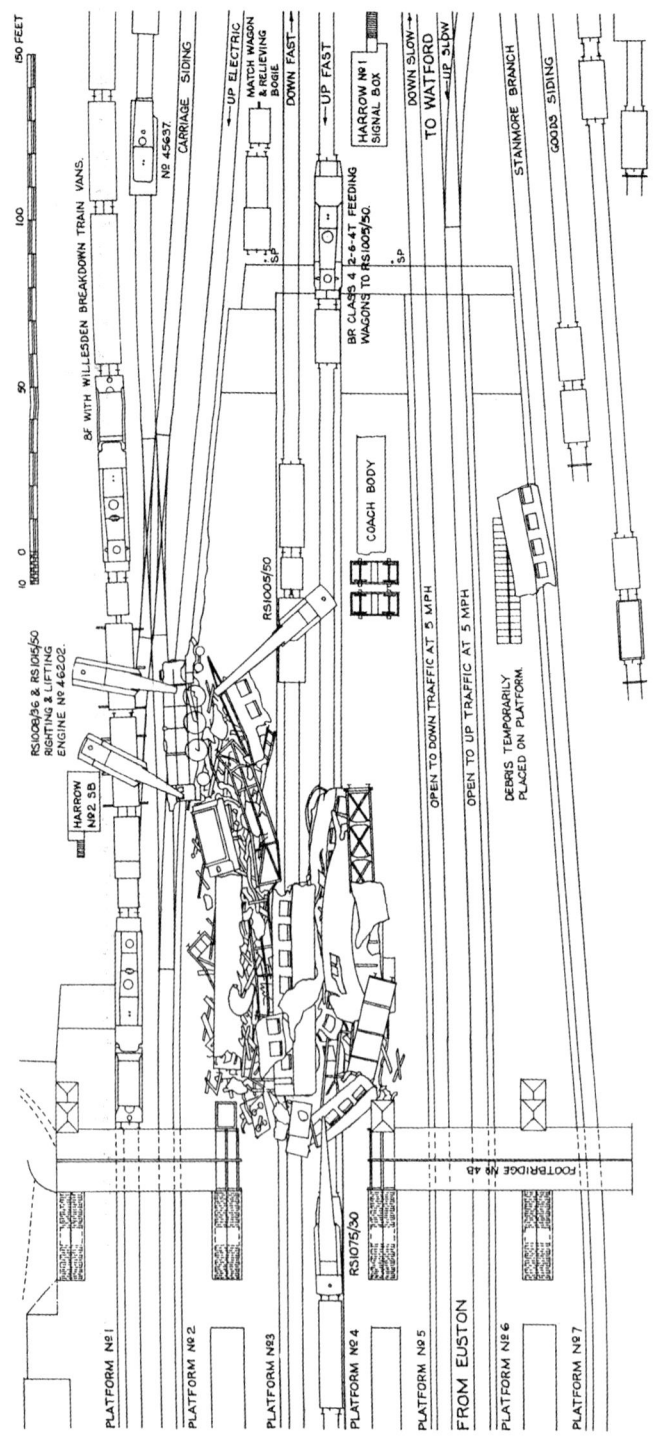

Figure 4: By early the following day the up and down slow lines have been reopened to traffic under a 5 mph speed restriction. The wreckage is being lifted off the fast lines by cranes at each end and another two, having removed the leading engine of the Liverpool/Manchester train, set about righting the train engine on the up electric line.

Author

A view of the scene of devastation, from the bracket signal beside down fast line at the platform end, looking south with the Rugby crane, partly obscured by the remnants of the coach of the Liverpool train, reaching out over platforms 4 and 5. The sixth coach of the Perth train is in the foreground. The coaches from the rest of the train, nearer the camera, have already been towed away. *Metropolitan Police Museum*

From an elevated position probably on the Willesden breakdown train, the photographer has captured the locomotives of the Liverpool and Manchester train, Nos. 45637 and 46202 lying on their sides on the up electric line, having been deflected across platforms 2 and 3 by the obstruction caused by the engine of the Perth train, No. 46242 derailed on the down fast line. *Metropolitan Police Museum*

With the aid of floodlights, work continued through the night, to recover the bodies of those killed and clear the wreckage from the line to enable the track and signalling to be restored prior to re-opening the line. The force of the impact on the leading engine of the Liverpool express, No. 45637, reduced it to little more than the boiler and that part of the frames carrying the driving wheels. Here the superheater header and motion brackets are to be seen as the Willesden and Kentish Town cranes lift the engine from the wreckage during the first night following the accident. *London Midland Region, BR*

This view was probably taken on the evening of 9th October, the second day, and shows another pair of steam breakdown cranes tackling the still very substantial pile of wreckage. The crane on the right is the Cowans Sheldon 50 ton No. RS1005/50 from Crewe on the down fast, while in the distance No. RS1075/30 from Rugby has moved over from the up slow, by now open to traffic, to the up fast. *Anthony V. Gregory*

A helmeted fireman speaks into the hand-held microphone of his 'walkie-talkie' radio supported on his back by his belt and straps over his shoulder. *Anthony V. Gregory*

A fireman directs his hose at some problem, possibly initiated by a stray spark from an oxy-acetylene burner cutting up metal debris.
Anthony V. Gregory

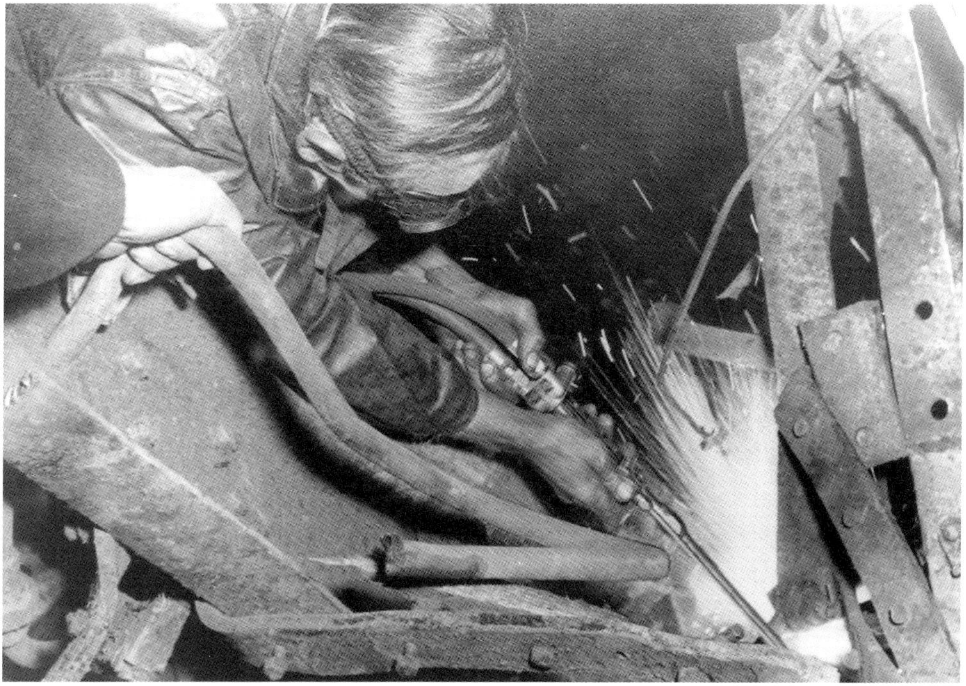

Above: A railway worker reaches down into the debris with his oxy-acetylene cutting touch, whilst a colleague holds a length of pipe clear, during the protracted process of clearing the huge pile of wreckage, resulting from the collision of three trains.

Anthony V. Gregory

Left: During the night, another worker, wearing goggles to prevent the glare causing his eyes to suffer from 'welder's flash', tackles part of some twisted coaches as sparks shower down.

Anthony V. Gregory

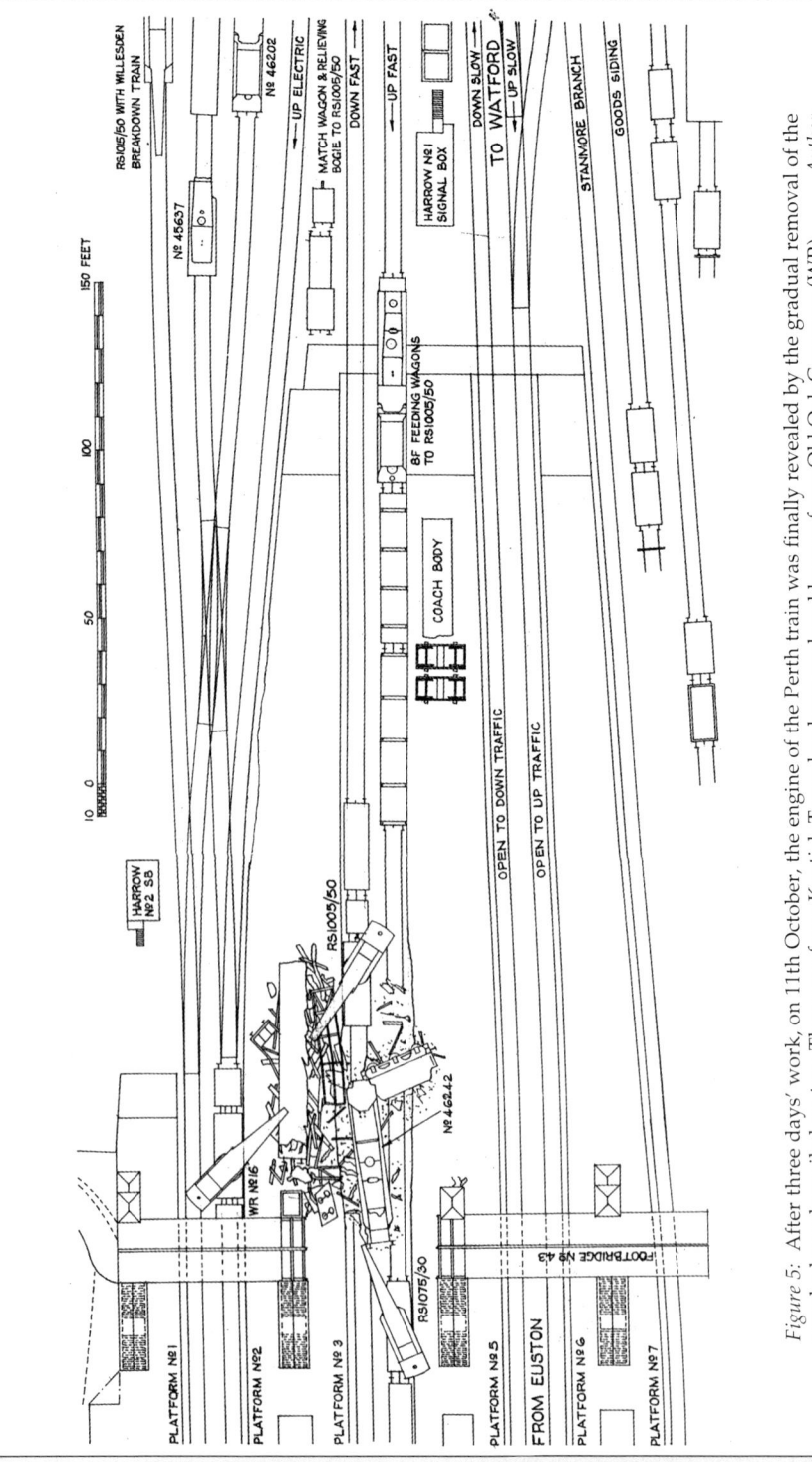

Figure 5: After three days' work, on 11th October, the engine of the Perth train was finally revealed by the gradual removal of the wrecked coaches piled on top. The crane from Kentish Town has been replaced by one from Old Oak Common (WR). *Author*

With cap on his head and cigarette in his mouth, but without goggles, a worker burns through a riveted steel member, probably from the station footbridge. Note the tilted coach in the left background. *Anthony V. Gregory*

Above: As the wreckage is cleared, officials are able to examine carefully the cab controls of No. 45637 as part of the meticulous investigation into the causes of the accident. *Anthony V. Gregory*

Left: In the second collision No. 45637, the leading engine of the Liverpool/Manchester train, took the full force of the impact against locomotive No. 46242 of the Perth train deflected into its path, following the first collision with the local train. No. 45637 ended up on its side with the whole of its front end demolished, including the right-hand side cylinder block. Here, before attempting to re-rail the engine, part of the bent-back connecting rod and piston is restrained by a rope as it is cut with an oxy-acetylene torch, while a Stanier 'Black Five' 4-6-0 waits with one of the breakdown trains in the background. *Anthony V. Gregory*

Above: For the first two days No. 46242 *City of Glasgow* of the Perth train remained totally obscured by the pile of debris it had caused by crashing into the local train and the subsequent colliding of the Liverpool/Manchester train. But by the third day the locomotive was finally unearthed from beneath the wreckage and is seen here looking down from the station footbridge.
London Midland Region, BR

Left: Another view of No. 46242. Remarkably, despite severe damage to the smokebox, frames and motion, this was the only of one the three wrecked engines to be repaired and restored to traffic. *Anthony V Gregory*

Left: Before the engine and tender of No. 46242 *City of Glasgow* could be righted and lifted onto the track to be drawn away into the goods yard siding, the lines up to and adjacent to them had to be cleared of debris to enable the cranes to approach close enough to work. Here the locomotive appears to have been restored to the rails with Crewe's 50 ton crane No. RS1005/50 standing in the background.
London Midland Region, BR

Below: No. 46242 *City of Glasgow* on Saturday 11th October, 1952. Note the damaged span of the footbridge and part of the station canopy removed to enable the cranes to operate freely, with onlookers standing on the barricaded off end, and the flood lights also mounted on the footbridge to illuminate night work. In the foreground a substantial quantity of debris and used gas bottles have still to be loaded up and carted away, including banana-shaped axles, wheels and twisted sections of carriage bogies.
W.S. Garth, Rail Archive Stephenson

before the engine and tender could be placed in the goods sidings, which required the crossing of both slow lines and was achieved at 4.05 pm. Following this, the up and down fast lines were cleared of debris. At 2.35 pm the Rugby breakdown train was reassembled on the up fast line and dispatched to Sudbury Jn, where it was re-marshalled, before returning to its depot. At the same time the Crewe breakdown train left the down fast line for its depot. The Willesden crane then moved from the goods yard to the down fast to load wagons placed on the up fast, until it departed at 1.40 am on 12th October. In the meantime a ballast train arrived on the up fast containing three 18 ft lengths of 15 in. diameter pipes with which to repair the burst Colne Valley water main. During the night, a Bakerloo Underground train trapped in the electric sidings was released. Further ballast trains arrived and departed loaded up with debris, while installation of a 6 ft wide temporary station footbridge commenced, signalling circuits were restored and fresh ballast placed in the fast lines. By the evening of Sunday 12th October the clearing of the line was substantially complete. The permanent way of the up and down fast lines was not very extensively damaged and after repairs had been carried out, traffic was restored by 8.00 pm after 4½ days. Normal working was then resumed with the speed restriction on the slow lines lifted and local trains resuming their calls at the station. A 15 mph speed restriction was, nonetheless, necessary on both the fast lines until 5.00 pm on 14th October while the track settled in. The reconstruction of the severely damaged platforms took until 6.00 pm on 13th October for the up fast and Monday morning 3rd November for the down fast. A temporary station footbridge was available for use by 9.30 pm on 12th October, and a new permanent span was installed on 9th November.

An accident of this magnitude involving over 1,000 passengers inevitably results in a very substantial amount of passengers' property and personal effects being scattered amongst all the other debris. Such matters were not overlooked, however, and arrangements were made for this to be collected in a central place under the custody of the police and returned to their rightful owners wherever possible against a written receipt. To this end motor lorries were commandeered from various goods depots in London, including two from the former Great Northern Railway depot at Edgware. A police guard was mounted over the mail vans until the GPO could make arrangements for the mail being transported by the trains to be collected from the scene and sent on its way by other means. All the letter mail and most of the parcel mail was recovered intact during the morning of the accident, although the contents of 23 parcels bags were delayed due to damage sustained. The blockage of the line, however, led to the introduction of a special temporary road service for mails to and from London until after the weekend. The first up special mail ran through on Monday morning, including the use of the mail bag apparatus in the vicinity of the station, which had not been damaged during the accident.

Later during the day of the accident the London Midland Region announced that it had awarded a contract to Tersons Ltd for the provision of, and subsequent removal of, a temporary footbridge and for permanent repairs to the footbridge No. 43, roofs, buildings and so on at Harrow & Wealdstone station. The new steelwork for the footbridge used modern welding techniques in place of the previous riveted construction.

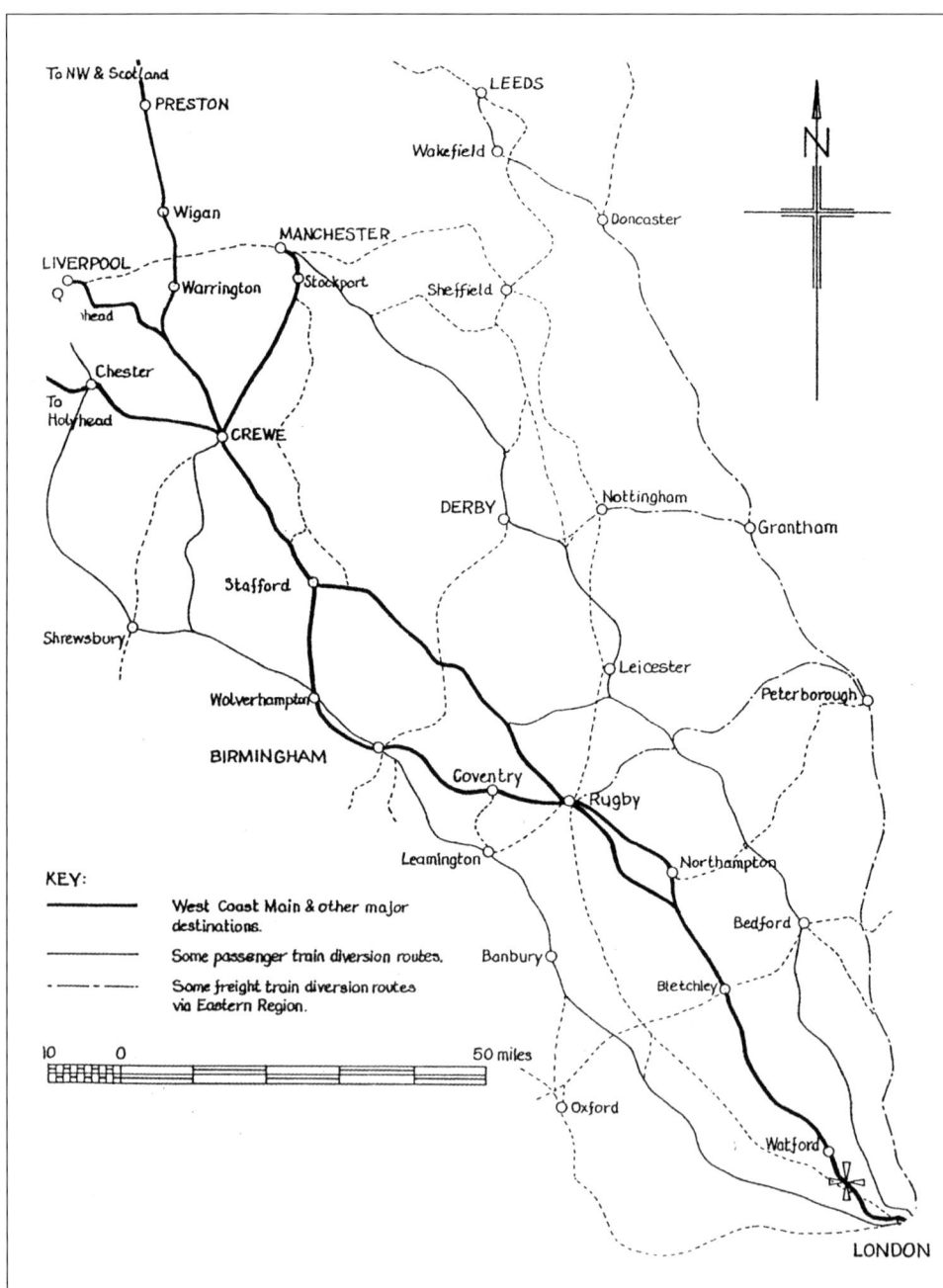

Figure 6: A map of the West Coast main line from London to Liverpool, Manchester and the North, with the adjacent lines showing the diversionary routes. *Author*

Disruption and Traffic Diversions

Total closure of the West Coast main line and electrified suburban line so close to its London terminal, led to widespread dislocation of traffic. Preparations made for aerial bombardment and experience gained during World War II enabled full use to be made of alternative routes. Most of Euston's passenger services were dealt with at St Pancras and Paddington, regaining the West Coast main line via Nuneaton and Wolverhampton respectively (*see Figure 6*). Other, generally shorter distance, trains were terminated and started at Watford Junction, passengers having to continue their journeys by the Metropolitan line, whilst a fair number of down passenger trains continued to depart from Euston and were sent via Willesden and Acton Wells to use the Midland division route as far as Nuneaton. Many special connecting services were run. For purely local journeys, buses were laid on between Wembley and Hatch End and Watford Junction and Watford Metropolitan stations, until electric services were restored. The buses were on hire from London Transport, which had two depots in Watford.

Control of rail traffic was exercised from District Control offices at Euston, St Pancras and Rugby, overseen by Divisional Control at Crewe, who will have liased with neighbouring divisions and other Regions. Horrendous as it undoubtedly was for the LMR Operating authorities, the Harrow & Wealdstone disaster was just another mishap, albeit on a grander scale. But, if one may say so, unlike the present day privatised railway they got on with the job of running a service, of sorts, rather than looking over their shoulders to see who might be taken to court.

In fact the LMS, later LMR, had a standard procedure which was brought into action as soon as a line was blocked and it was anticipated that the blockage would persist for some time. This included standing instructions about diversions whatever the cause of the obstruction to the line. On certain routes improvements were carried out to render them suitable as diversionary routes and many engine sheds had odd workings over unusual routes so that crews could maintain their route knowledge in anticipation of the need to operate diverted and excursion trains.

Here, with all lines blocked south of Bletchley, North Wales, Liverpool and North services were in the past usually diverted to St Pancras via Wigston Magna and Nuneaton. In LMS days, however, the Birmingham trains would have been a different matter, as there was little point in paying the Great Western Railway a significant sum per train mile to have them run LMS trains into Paddington when the customers, as soon as they realised there was a risk of serious delay, voted with their feet anyway by taking the GW train, so many Birmingham and Wolverhampton trains would have been simply cancelled. As for Manchester passengers, tickets could simply be made available via Derby and extra trains were laid on as required. In both cases, however, since the engine route availability did not permit Stanier Pacifics into St Pancras, 4-6-0s would be in demand, while since Nationalisation Paddington could be used without undue penalty.

There were previously prepared contingency plans laid down to cover blockages on all sections of the line. Between Crewe and Stafford diversion was via Shrewsbury, between Crewe and Warrington it was via Chester or via Manchester and Springs Branch and so on. Prior to Nationalisation, one of the worst bits was a blockage between Bletchley and Roade, as diversion via

Verney Junction involving travelling very slowly for quite long distances on country branches was hardly a viable option. Inevitably arrival in Crewe would be very late, but the LMS/LMR eventually got one home.

In such cases there was no time to produce Special Traffic Notices and Control was in its element. The overall plan to be adopted was agreed by Divisional Control, in conjunction with Derby, Manchester and Glasgow or even other companies or Regions as appropriate, and details such as motive power, rosters, reliefs and so on, were handled by District Control Offices. The controllers and specialist operating staff such as district inspectors really came into their own at times like this. In fact it has taken several years of quasi-privatisation followed by the real thing for it to dawn on people just how professional the much-maligned railway operators were.

In this case upon receipt of the news of the accident and the extent of the blockage, Mr A. Lawrence at Euston Control Room notified the District Operating Superintendent, Mr L.W. Cox, who promptly left for Harrow & Wealdstone station, where as previously mentioned he worked in the temporary control point set up in a waiting room with other senior officers who had travelled on the local train. He established contact by railway telephone with his deputy, Mr C.R. Bennett, who remained in charge at Euston. Amongst those quickly informed by Control of the accident were the Accident Section, Personal Injuries Section and the Hotel Executive, who were asked to provide food and drinks for the injured and rescuers at the scene. Control also gave directions to every signal box in the district. Important freight, perishables and livestock, together with mail was given priority over less urgent freight traffic which was temporarily shunted into sidings. At 11.00 am a telephone conference was held between the 11 districts affected between London and Carlisle to arrange the various diversions and arrangements to handle the traffic diverted away from the scene of the accident.

Passengers on those overnight and local trains already south of Bletchley were seriously delayed while their trains were terminated at Watford Junction, with onward journeys by bus or the Metropolitan line to Baker Street. Those trains at, or north of, Bletchley were worked either to Paddington or St Pancras. To a lineside viewer at Kings Langley, north of Watford, one of the first signs of trouble on the line was the sight of a Pacific locomotive at 10.43 am running tender first through the station with the empty stock off the 5.15 pm overnight train from Inverness, complete with sleeping cars. In the other direction the Rugby breakdown train was observed heading south for the scene of the accident. Other strange sights included a 'Princess' class in reverse hauling a rake of local stock in the down direction. In addition to parcels and Engineer's trains, the local trains from the north seemed to have run to and from Watford Jn, together with a couple of trains from Wolverhampton, passengers having to complete their journeys to the Metropolis by London Transport. Some long distance north-bound evening departures were made from Watford Jn, including at 10.20 pm a Pacific-hauled Stranraer boat train and at 11.15 pm (9.35 pm ex-Euston) of six coaches to Birmingham behind a rebuilt 'Scot'. Elsewhere on the system some, such as the booking clerk at Radlett, only became aware that there was a major problem when diverted trains started to pass through on his line.

Initially a total of 16 departures from Euston, together with three more shortly after midnight, were worked round to the Midland main line by diverging at Willesden

Junction onto the goods lines to Acton Wells Jn, where they were reversed to proceed to Brent Jn, Cricklewood, while later four departures were made from St Pancras, *see Appendix Two*. To eliminate working passenger trains over goods lines, with the need to clip and padlock facing points, and all the complications of turn over engines necessary at the point of the reversal of trains that this involved, within a few hours of the disaster, arrangements were put in hand for a number of LMR long distance trains to be diverted to other London Termini. Hurriedly prepared blackboards were placed on display at all London stations announcing the interruption to services. Subsequently specially printed bills were displayed on easel boards detailing the special emergency arrangements put in hand, including the revised starting points in London of trains scheduled to have departed from Euston and alternative routes to stations to Watford Junction. At Euston passengers intending to sail on SS *Freemantle* were advised to go to Paddington and travel to Birkenhead. Likewise passengers for Birmingham and Wolverhampton were also directed to Paddington, while those for Manchester were advised to try St Pancras. The first train to leave Euston after the crash was the 8.30 am to Liverpool which steamed out more than an hour late, while the 12.00 noon train to the same destination left from Watford Jn, and the 12.40 pm to Wolverhampton was cancelled. Passengers for the 9.45 am 'Comet' to Manchester and 10.00 am 'Royal Scot' to Glasgow were told that they would travel by Acton Wells and Cricklewood and therefore would be liable to heavy delays while the procedure described above was carried out.

In this way an observer at Luton noted the first out of course working of rebuilt 'Patriot' class No. 45530 *Sir Frank Ree* at 12.25 pm with a down train for Manchester, followed 13 minutes later by 'Jubilee' class No. 45553 *Canada* on the down 'Comet'. At 12.55 pm No. 45519 *Lady Godiva* passed on an unidentified train and No. 46168 *The Girl Guide* of the rebuilt 'Royal Scot' class on the 'Royal Scot' train at 1.05 pm. As well as numerous 'Scots' and a couple of 'Patriots', No. 45734 *Meteor* passed Luton at 12.52 pm with the 7.50 am from Wolverhampton; followed by class 'Five' No. 45381 at 1.10 pm with the up 'Ulster Express' from Heysham; No. 46140 *The King's Royal Rifle Corps* on the up 'Royal Scot' at 8.15 pm; No. 46147 *The Northamptonshire Regiment* with an up Manchester train at 8.04 pm; and rebuilt 'Patriot' class No. 45526 *Morecambe and Heysham* with the 12.45 pm from Bangor at 8.32 pm. In the down direction some of the empty stock returned on the down 'Midday Scot' behind No. 45573 *Newfoundland*; No. 46132 *The King's Regiment (Liverpool)* passed through at 4.12 pm with a train for Liverpool; while No. 45734 returned with the down 'Ulster Express' to Heysham at 6.12 pm.

At Dudding Hill Jn, on the diversion route from the Western to Midland main lines of the LMR, No. 46169 *The Boy Scout* of Longsight was noted at 8.05 pm running from Welsh Harp towards Willesden with the empty corridor stock carrying coach destination boards inscribed 'Liverpool-London', together with one 'Inverness-London'. Fifty minutes later No. 46119 *Lancashire Fusilier* shedded at Holyhead, ran tender first in the direction of Kentish Town with empty sleeping car stock for Glasgow otherwise intended for the 9.10 pm from Euston. This train returning passed Cricklewood at about 10.45 pm heading north at speed behind No. 46141 *The North Staffordshire Regiment* of Camden. At 9.20 pm rebuilt 'Patriot' class No. 45514 *Holyhead*, also allocated to Camden, was observed hauling the 7.30 pm Euston to Perth sleeper train from Acton Wells towards Welsh Harp and the North.

These diversions continued early the next day, with No. 45599 *Bechuanaland* arriving at St Pancras with an overnight sleeping car train. The slow lines through Harrow had been restored, however, from that morning thereby reducing the need for diversions the following day to five down and three up trains, including the overnight train on 9th/10th October from Perth (8.15 pm), which worked to St Pancras, together with those to and from Wolverhampton which operated out of Paddington.

With 19 West Coast route expresses arrivals handled at St Pancras that first day, Paddington was also brought in to share the load, as shown in *Appendix Two*. Note how several down trains relied on stock which had been brought in by up trains. In the up direction the 8.00 am from Blackpool Central and 7.30 am from Holyhead had already been combined at Crewe into a 15-coach train as part of the existing temporary measures to curtail movements at Euston due to track alterations taking place there in connection with re-signalling work. It left Crewe 20 minutes late and travelled behind No. 45736 *Atlas* via Nantwich, Market Drayton and Wellington to Wolverhampton (Low Level), where WR 'County' class 4-6-0 No. 1016 *County of Hants* took over, leaving at 12.40 pm for the rest of the journey to Paddington via Birmingham (Snow Hill), arriving at 3.40 pm 2½ hours late into London. The stock was worked back as the 5.50 pm departure to Blackpool and Holyhead, via Bushbury and Stafford. Both the 8.10 am and 10.10 am from Liverpool also came via Market Drayton, the latter arriving at Paddington behind WR 'Castle' class 4-6-0 No. 4092 *Dunraven Castle*. These two trains returned at 5.00 pm and 7.12 pm from Paddington via Bushbury Jn and Stafford. The 9.45 am from Wolverhampton and Birmingham arrived via Coventry, Kenilworth and Leamington Spa and went back at 6.08 pm, whereas the empty stock off the 11.55 am from Wolverhampton was returned to Willesden via Kensington. No. 45595 *Southern Rhodesia* with the 9.45 am 'Mancunian' of 12 coaches from Manchester via Market Drayton relinquished its train to WR 'Hall' class 4-6-0 No. 4960 *Pyle Hall* at Wolverhampton (Low Level) and the train returned to Manchester as the 6.23 pm, also via Bushbury and Stafford.

In the down direction a relief to the Western Region's 11.10 am train from Paddington to Birkenhead was run at 10.56 am, calling at Birmingham (Snow Hill) and Wolverhampton Low Level (LL), whilst passengers for the White Star Line were accommodated on the 11.10 am to Birkenhead. The next day, Thursday 9th October, four down trains ran from Paddington, including the 12.50 pm for Liverpool behind 'Star' class 4-6-0 No. 4053 *Princess Alexandra* shedded at Stafford Road and the 1.00 pm for Wolverhampton, which departing 18 minutes later behind 'Grange' class 4-6-0 No. 6859 *Yiewsley Grange* from Birkenhead shed. The 4.30 pm to Liverpool arrived at Snow Hill behind No. 5912 *Queen's Hall* and 6979 *Helperly Hall* with 15 coaches and was announced over the loudspeaker to call at Wolverhampton LL and Crewe. Rebuilt 'Patriot' class No. 45527 *Southport* took over from WR motive power at Wolverhampton. At Snow Hill No. 1003 *County of Wilts* passed through on the middle road in the up direction with 13 coaches with, it was thought, the 4.10 pm from Liverpool, presumably omitting its call at Rugby. No. 1016 *County of Hants* hauled the 15 coaches of the combined 5.15 pm to Holyhead and 5.05 pm to Blackpool, assisted between Leamington and Wolverhampton by 2-6-2T No. 5185 marshalled inside. They were relieved at Wolverhampton by No. 45736 *Phoenix*. The up 'Midlander' arrived at Paddington at 1.30 pm behind No. 7927 *Willington Hall* of Stafford Road and the train of 10 coaches returned hauled by No. 5954 *Faendre Hall* to Wolverhampton LL after which it conveyed the stock on to Cannock Road (WR) sidings for disposal. For the subsequent three days, however, this train ran to Wolverhampton (High Level) via New Street, Coventry and Leamington Spa. The down 'Mancurian' arrived at Wolverhampton LL behind No. 4960 *Pyle Hall* with 12 coaches and handed over to 'Jubilee' class No. 45595 *Southern Rhodesia*, whilst the 15-coach 'Merseyside Express', with through coaches for Southport, was double-headed by No. 6874 *Haughton Grange* and No. 4092 *Aldenham Hall* and taken forward by another Jubilee No. 45634 *Trinidad*. On Friday the 1.00 pm to Wolverhampton was hauled by No. 6013 *King Henry VIII*. All these extra trains imposed on top of the Western Region's regular services, to say nothing of the demands for extra motive power, placed a strain on the system and many domestic trains, mainly in the down direction, were delayed, typically by ½ to ¾ hour, as a consequence. Perhaps for this reason and possibly as the LMR unravelled the passenger and freight trains held up by the line blockage at Harrow, later trains diverted from the West Coast main line to Paddington travelled via Nuneaton, Coventry and Leamington Spa.

The Thursday also resulted in the arrival of a scheduled boat train from Liverpool behind No. 5066 *Wardour Castle* with passengers from SS *Franconia*. By Friday, however, only two trains in each direction used Paddington. During this period most LMR stock was serviced at Old Oak Common or West London carriage sidings with occasional transfers to the West Coast main line via Mitre Bridge and the West London line. LMR locomotives seem to have worked trains from the North to Wolverhampton Low Level via either Cannock Road Jn, or Wellington, where WR motive power took over. As a result several LMR engines, including Nos. 44907, 45527, 45578, 45595 and 45634, appeared at Stafford Road shed.

Four parcels trains were diverted via the Western Region on the day of the accident, three on 9th October and just one the day following. Many freight services had to be cancelled or diverted with consequent disruption of the working of Willesden and other yards and goods stations. Two freight trains conveying meat from Carlisle travelled by way of the Midland main line and Acton Wells to Broad Street, whilst a fish train from Fleetwood went via Kentish Town and the North London line. Several trains of empty mineral wagons from the Southern Region for the Midlands were sent by way of Reading, instead of Willesden.

With the co-operation of other Regions, however, diversions and improvised arrangements were implemented, thus preventing serious congestion, and the traffic position was restored to normal by Monday, 13th October. Those diverted via Eastern Region lines between 8th and 10th October are also listed in *Appendix Two*, together with a fish train from Aberdeen usually routed up the West Coast main line which was diverted to Kings Cross. Many LMR engines, including Nos. 44831, 45131, 45321, 45379 and 45438, worked up ER lines as far as Canonbury, whilst on the 8th October ER engines, mostly from Peterborough, hauled all down trains. On two occasions these included the 'A1' from Grantham off the up 'White Rose', which normally worked back light engine. Subsequently LMR engines and crews worked the first three trains through with ER pilot men, while only one train ran via the ER on Saturday night 11th October.

On the electric lines, to enable the passengers to be cleared from the trains brought to a stand between Harrow and Hatch End, it was necessary shortly after 9 o'clock to extend the isolation of traction power as far as Wembley Central. Once this was completed, current was restored again between 10.22 am and 11.22 am to enable three electric trains standing on the up line between Hatch End and Harrow to be worked back 'wrong line' to Croxley Green and clear the line for use by breakdown cranes. On the Wembley side of the accident, six trains were standing on the up line between Harrow & Wealdstone and Wembley and five on the down line. The conductor rails were made live again at 11.22 am to enable these trains to be worked clear and on to Queens Park, after which power was isolated at 2.25 pm to enable the Kentish Town crane to proceed to the site from Stonebridge Power Station.

London Underground Bakerloo and LMR electric multiple unit services were suspended between Watford Jn and Queens Park at 8.33am. Bakerloo trains were either turned round at Queens Park, or those scheduled to terminate at Wembley were diverted to Stanmore instead. Later a service of four LMR electric trains was reinstated from London to Wembley Central and from Hatch End to Watford Jn, while every half-hour one of the latter ran to Kenton over the up electric line under single line working utilising a pilotman. Between 3.00 pm and 7.00 pm an additional two trains per hour were operated from Broad Street to Wembley and back. On Thursday and Friday a similar service was operated with an additional two trains on the Broad Street run between 5.00 am and 10.00 am and the Watford to Hatch End service was increased to six per hour between 4.30 am and 10.00 am and 3.00 pm to 7.00 pm. By Saturday morning normal service was resumed. The reintroduction of services on London Underground's Bakerloo line was somewhat more protracted with only three trains at Watford, which set off early on the Saturday morning and thereafter those services due to terminate at Harrow did so at Queens Park until the berthing sidings were cleared over a month later.

To fill the gap, a bus service was instituted by the London Transport Executive, Central Road Services between these two stations. This started at 8.55 am under the supervision of Inspector Slade with 16 buses, later increased to 15 calling at all stations between Wembley and Hatch End, while another 10 worked direct between the two, calling only at Harrow. Finally 54 buses were utilised in the rush hour, with up to six vehicles at one time loading at Wembley Central station. The next day 50 were employed on the direct service and 15 on the intermediate service, with spare buses being held in reserve at Edgware garage. There was an increase in passenger movement from Edgware station necessitating five extra buses on route 18 to Wembley and five more buses on route 142 between Stanmore, Bushey and Watford, rail passengers to Bushey being directed to use the Stanmore line. Alternatively passengers for Watford Jn, Tring etc. could use the Metropolitan line to Watford, from where an emergency bus service was operated by London Transport Country Services to Watford Jn, together with road vans shuttling back and forth with passengers' luggage (*see Figure 7, page 90*). On the Metropolitan line, trains scheduled to run non-stop between Eastcote to Finchley Road in the morning peak period or Finchley Road to Eastcote or North Harrow in the evening rush hour, called additionally at Harrow on the Hill. Outer suburban main line services to Tring and Northampton left from Watford Jn.

The position was eased when the slow lines at Harrow & Wealdstone were opened to traffic early the next day, Thursday 9th October, and five up and one down train passed through in the first hour, including overnight trains from Glasgow and Manchester, the Tring to Euston local which did not stop and the early morning train to Windermere. Later in the day, those known to have passed the site of the accident were the 4.30 pm to Liverpool; 4.37 pm to Wolverhampton; 6.07 pm to Liverpool and 6.20 pm to Preston. Local bookings were accepted at the station and passengers directed straight onto special buses outside the station, which took them to Wembley or Hatch End as appropriate to pick up trains. Some long distance overnight trains called additionally at Watford Jn about 30 minutes after leaving Euston to pick up passengers, thereby avoiding the need of those from the northern suburbs to make a difficult journey to and through London. On Thursday/Friday 9th/10th October, these trains included 7.20 pm 'Royal Highlander' to Inverness; 7.30 pm to Perth; 8.45 pm 'Irish Mail' to Holyhead; 9.10 pm and 9.25 pm to Glasgow; 10.52 pm to Perth; 11.15 pm to Windermere; 11.40 pm 'Night Scot' to Glasgow; 12.02 am to Crewe; 12.20 am to Manchester; and 12.30 am to Liverpool. Nonetheless, some diversions were still necessary until the fast lines could be opened again on 12th October. Three days later the Queen returning to London in the Royal Train passed slowly through and under the temporary footbridge behind No. 46245 *City of London*, as final repairs to the platforms continued.

Spiritual and Psychological Aspects

Revd John D. Richards, Vicar of St John Baptist Parish Church, Greenhill, Harrow was one of many clergymen of the neighbourhood who made their way that morning to minister to the wounded and rescuers. In the afternoon he and Revd Roy Deasy, his senior curate, climbed in a car and toured a number of hospitals visiting and comforting the injured and then returned to the scene. The Revd H.E. Stewart, Vicar of Holy Trinity, Wealdstone moved among the more seriously injured, while the Revd M. Evelyn, in charge of a nearby preparatory school, administered the Holy Sacrament dressed in vestments. The Revd K.T. Toole-Mackson, Vicar of St Anselm's, Belmont, went to Edgware General Hospital to support the injured. Also on the scene were Father George Barrington of All Saints, Kenton, together with Fathers Leonard Egen and Eugene Gallagher, curates of St Joseph's Harrow and Wealdstone who had been told of the crash by pupils of their college. Two nuns from the Convent of the Sacred Heart Grammar School at Wealdstone waited on the platform in case any of their children were found under the debris. The Revd Philip Savage of Hatch End Free Church joined the railway padre to tour the hospitals to comfort the injured. Later in the day the Bishop of Willesden came to see the scene for himself and made arrangements for at least one clergyman to be on hand at the station until the last casualty was recovered to administer the last sacrament if necessary.

There were many memorial services for the victims and thanksgiving for those who survived. *The Times* newspaper reports one on the station platform on 12th October, 1952, when work was interrupted for prayers on the platform conducted

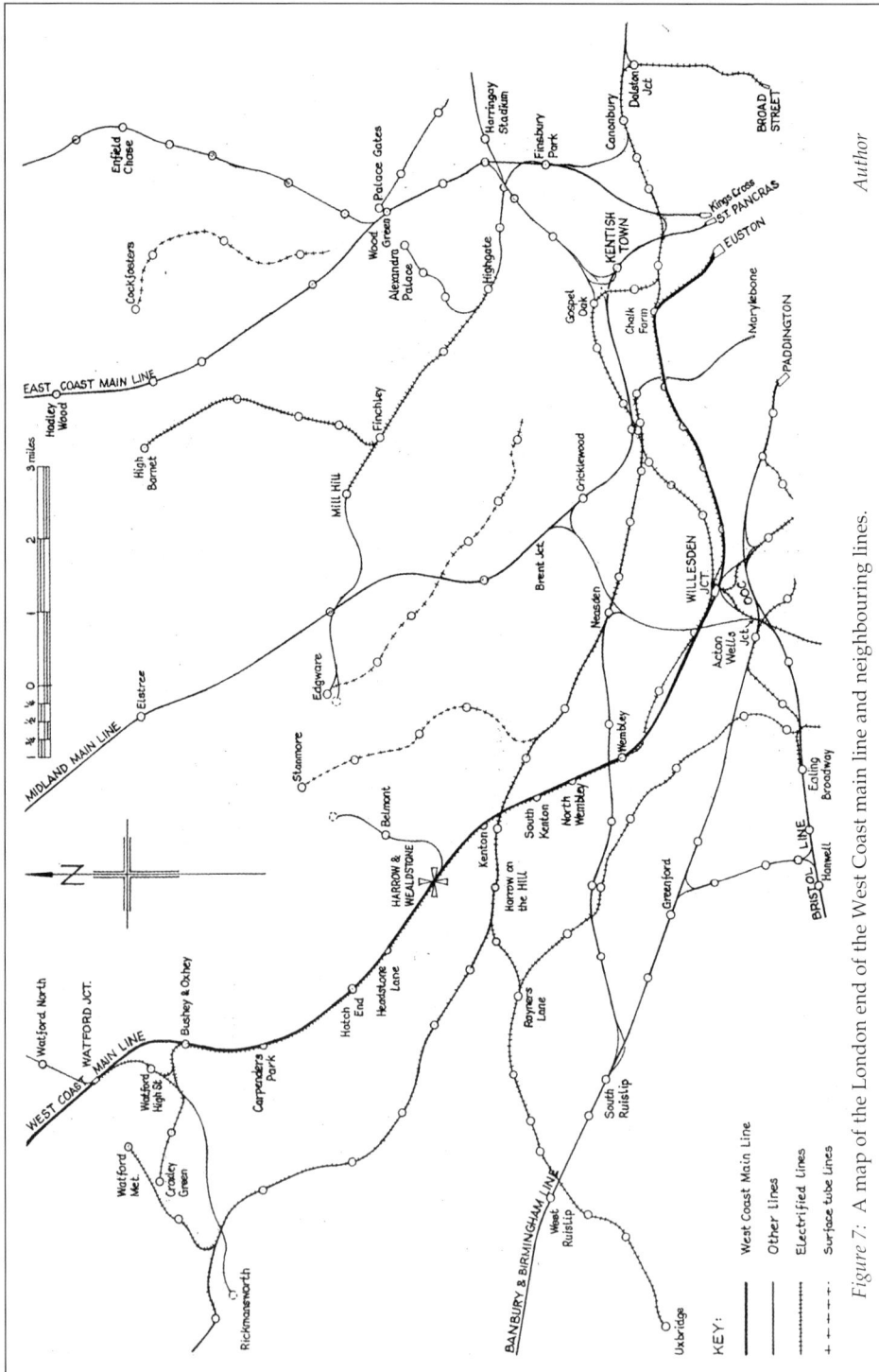

Figure 7: A map of the London end of the West Coast main line and neighbouring lines.

by Revd Arthur Oldham, whilst memorial services were held the same day at St Michael's Harrow Weald, conducted by Revd J.H. Morris. Special prayers were said at All Saints' Harrow Weald and St Barnabas' Church on the Cedars Estate. The next day a requiem mass was celebrated at St Aloysius Roman Catholic Church, Eversholt St, London NW1 attended by Cardinal Griffin, the Roman Catholic Archbishop of Westminster, whilst on 15th October at 8.00 pm the Bishop of London conducted a service at Holy Trinity, Wealdstone assisted by the Vicar and free church ministers. This was relaid to a neighbouring hall for those who could not be accommodated in the church and broadcast over the radio on the Light Programme. Another was held at St Anselm's Belmont on Friday 17th October conducted by Revd K.T. Toole-Mackson and again by Revd A. Binney on the following Sunday 19th October at the Methodist Church in nearby Locket Road, whose congregation had lost two members killed and many injured. Several funerals took place during the week. On Sunday 26th at 3.00 pm the Bishop of St Albans led a service in St Mary's, Watford parish church, organised by Watford Borough Council, for the dead in the Watford and King's Langley area, including a member of their choir. The church building was packed and loudspeakers relaid the service to those outside.

A memorial service for railway employees whose lives were lost and a thanksgiving service for those who lives were spared, held at 11.30 am on Thursday 23rd October at St Marylebone Parish Church, London NW1, drew a congregation of 1,500 people. Admission was by ticket only and attended by senior officials of the British Transport Commission and Railway Executive, by Chief Regional Officers and many grades of railwaymen were represented. The service was conducted by Revd W.P. Baddeley, the Vicar of St Pancras, with Revd John Richards from Harrow leading the prayers and J. Taylor Thompson, the Chief Engineer of the LMR, reading the lesson. In his address the Right Reverend Joost de Blank, Lord Bishop of Stepney and formerly Vicar of St John the Baptist, Harrow, firstly gave thanks for the faithful service rendered by those who work on the railway and those who undertook rescue work. Secondly, in consoling those who had lost loved ones, he offered thanks for their lives whilst on earth and for hope in the Resurrection. It is understood that for a number of years, wreaths were laid on the platform on the anniversary of the accident.

On the day of the accident, as a result of enquiries received, Charles E. Jordan JP, Chairman of Harrow Urban District Council, launched the Railway Disaster Fund to relieve cases of hardship caused by the accident.

A great deal of pain was incurred by the survivors and those involved in clearing the site, caused by the certain knowledge that the accident involved close friends and maybe in a few cases relatives. Permanent way staff, being the largest group of men to hand in an emergency, and other workers became brutalised, as they took the full brunt, working with undertakers' staff to pick up human remains. One can imagine the feelings of the men, as human tissue continued to be found up to the last stages of clearing the site. Others were affected because they should ordinarily have been on the train, but for some reason, such as illness, missed it or caught an earlier one or went for a later train. A year later many were still coping with the aftermath. Forty-three railway staff from Euston and BTC HQ travelling on the local train lost their lives. Twenty-seven homes in Watford lost someone, whilst another 40 now had a member of the household injured.

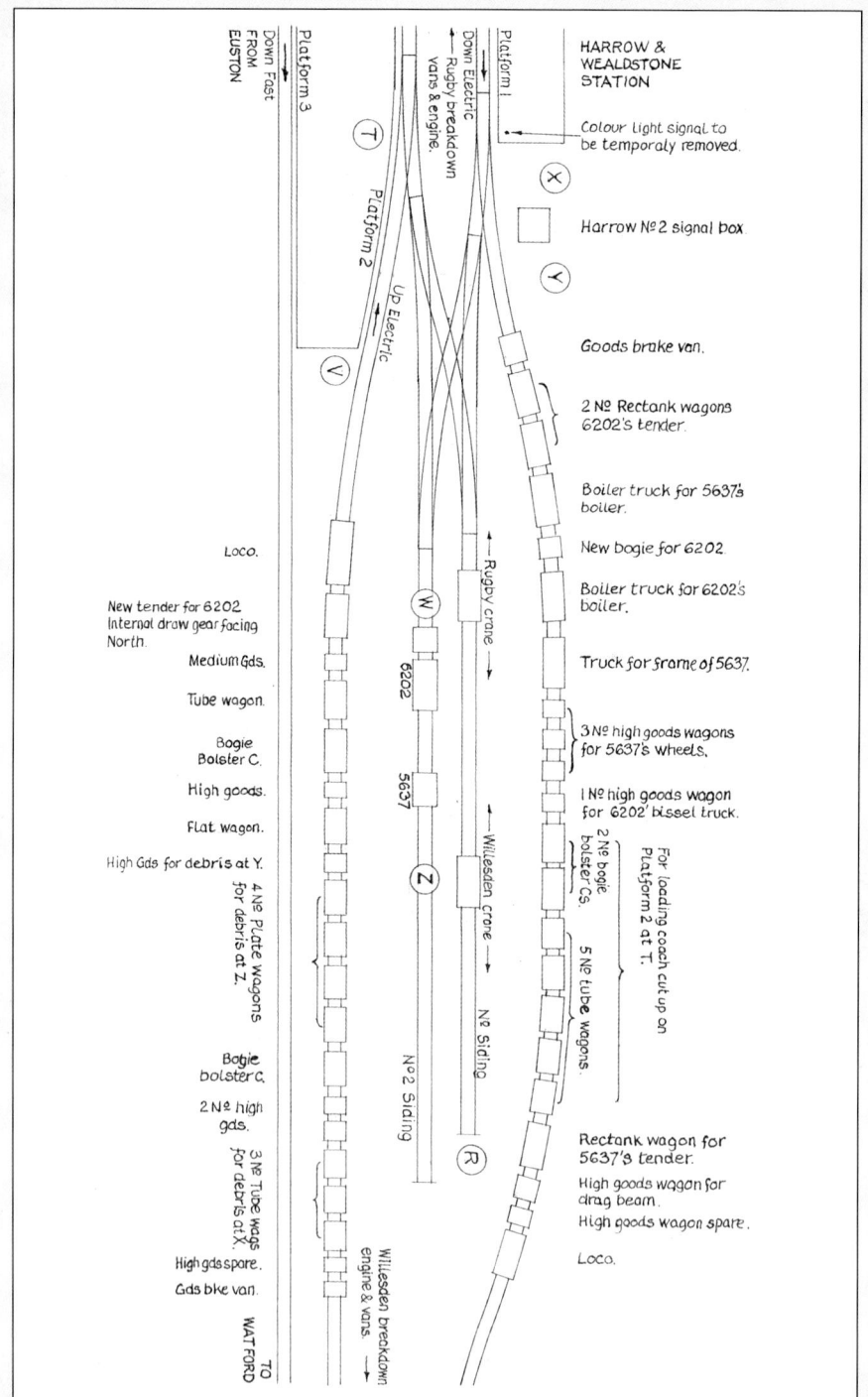

Figure 8: A diagram of the formation of the material trains for the recovery operation of locomotive Nos. 45637 *Windward Islands* and 46202 *Princess Anne* on 9th November, 1952.   *Author*

Subsequent Clearing Up Operations

After examination, locomotives Nos. 45637, 46202 and 46242 were sheeted over and left until removed the next month. In preparation for the recovery operation planned for 8th/9th November, a site meeting was held on 22nd October and a further meeting was called by the Works Superintendent at Crewe for 24th October attended by 21 representatives of various departments to make arrangements for the recovery of the locomotives. It was proposed to deal with No. 45637 piecemeal, while No. 46202 required to have a new bogie fitted to enable the chassis to be taken away on its own wheels coupled to a new tender. The tender to No. 46242 was to be loaded up and a fresh tender provided to enable the remains of this engine, after certain straightening of the frames, changing of the wheels and possible removal of certain parts, to be hauled to Crewe.

In view of the long planned heavy engineering works in November and December, it was subsequently decided that priority must be given to dealing with the two engines in the electric sidings in a single weekend possession from 1.30 am on Sunday to 4.00 am on Monday, i.e. after the last electric train on Saturday/Sunday night to first train on Monday morning. In addition, 'in between trains' possession of the down fast was to be operated by flagmen while lifting on the adjacent electric line was taking place. Even so, this meant postponing the track relaying on the up and down slow lines between Sudbury and Harrow. In view of the length of this operation, sufficient manpower to permit a shift system to operate was recognised and a request was made for a third class sleeping car, or failing that an ordinary coach, to be placed in the goods yard to afford proper rest for those off duty, rather than use the breakdown riding vans which would be too close to noisy activities and those taking meals. Opportunity was also taken on 2nd November, while the District Engineer had possession of the up and down fast lines to replace the damaged portion of the station footbridge, for the Willesden crane to load up some heavy debris lying between the tracks south of the station. Further amounts of smaller debris in various locations was to be loaded into wagons by local arrangement.

Commencing on 28th October, some preparatory work had been undertaken by cutting back projecting items with oxy-acetylene torches, until No. 45637 consisted only of the boiler and frame mounted on the six driving wheels, and nothing else. Even the last of any of the remaining green-painted cladding to the boiler was removed. The components of its tender tank were reduced sufficiently to be within gauge. Likewise the tank of No. 46202 was separated from the frames, the chimney taken off and the rear of the engine's outer frames, which were badly out of gauge, cut off and the buffer beam made suitable for coupling up in advance of the weekend by staff from Crewe locomotive works. The men necessary for the advanced work were accommodated in the enginemen's hostel and a midday meal provided from Willesden canteen. Meticulous preparations were made for assembling the two materials trains, their shunting and positioning on site and the precise order of each lift predetermined to avoid congestion on the constricted site (*see Figure 8*).

During an operation over the weekend of 8th/9th November to recover Nos. 45637 and 46202, the service between Harrow and the Watford Jn was maintained

Left: Such of the floor of the cab that survived and the drawplate of No. 45637 was twisted at an angle, whilst the entire cab structure was demolished. *London Midland Region, BR*

Above right: Re-railed and temporarily placed in one of the electric berthing sidings, on 10th October the sorry state of No. 46202 *Princess Anne* is apparent, with its front bogie and motion on the left-hand side ripped away as the locomotive, turned on its side by the collision, rode over the station platform to land on the up electric line. *H.C. Casserley*

Right: In the electric train berthing sidings Willesden's 50 ton crane No. RS1015/50 attends to No. 46202 preparing a 'jury rig', while in the foreground various wheels and coach underframes wait to be recovered.
Author's Collection

No. 45637 was so severely wrecked that only the boiler, firebox and the frames supporting the three driving axles, plus the rear frames remained. Much of the cladding and all of the motion was torn away as she collided with No. 46242, which had strayed into her path after hitting the rear of the local train. She is seen here temporarily placed in the electric berthing sidings awaiting removal and inevitable scrapping. . *London Midland Region, BR*

Still without its leading driving wheel set and rear pony truck, the frames of No. 46202 are seen with a leading bogie in place with two cranes in attendance.

Locofotos, J.A.G.H. Coltas Collection courtesy H.N. Twells

No. 46242 *City of Glasgow* was removed to the station goods yard on the up side, where during the week following the battered state of the locomotive was recorded by the official photographer, minus cylinder and all motion, boiler fittings, together with other parts.

London Midland Region, BR

A close up of the cab and the front of the tender showing how the footplatemen must have been crushed as the tender and the following train drove into the engine and slewed round.

London Midland Region, BR

Stanier 'Black Five' No. 45252 returning home on the down slow line with Crewe's breakdown train, including 50 ton crane RS1005/50 near Headstone Lane late on Saturday, 11th October, after one of the longest jobs in its history. *D. Lawrence*

all day on Sunday by a shuttle service operating on the slow lines and utilising the two-coach auto-fitted set and locomotives Nos. 40010, 40043, 41220 and 41275, the first three locomotives and the coaches normally sharing in the working between Harrow and Belmont. This service was supplemented by buses for those stations without platforms on the slow lines, such as Headstone Lane.

The breakdown cranes from Willesden (RS1015/50) and Rugby (RS1075/30) were positioned on the electric siding No. 1 and manoeuvred along these under their own power, as required. Materials trains made up of a number of wagons of special types, including some trolleys, tubes and open wagons were brought in (*see Figure 8*), being shunted up and down the electric lines to near the load to be lifted. By about 8.00 am the next morning the boiler of No. 45637 had been removed from the main frames and loaded on a 35 ton bogie Rectank wagon. The wheel sets were separated from the frames and loaded into open wagons, while the frames were then placed by the Rugby crane onto another Rectank wagon, after which all was drawn away at 11.10 am by Stanier 2-8-0 No. 48601. In

Likewise Willesden's breakdown train with 50 ton crane No. RS1015/50 is on the move between the scene of the accident and its depot behind Stanier 2-8-0 class '8F' No. 48550.
Don Coventry

Following the last train on Saturday 7th November, the electric services were suspended while Nos. 45637 and 46202 were removed. The remnants of No. 45637 were dismantled into its major constituent parts and loaded into wagons to be transported away to Crewe works. In this view the severely battered frames are lifted off the driving wheels by Rugby's 30 ton crane No. RS1075/30, while Stanier 2-8-0 class '8F' No. 48601 waits on an adjacent track with a materials train into which the frame will be loaded. *London Midland Region, BR*

As it was Remembrance Sunday, there was a pause in the proceedings with hats off and heads bowed during the act of remembrance. Subsequently work will have continued loading the driving wheels into the adjacent materials train. *London Midland Region, BR*

On Sunday 16th November the Willesden 50 ton crane was used to separate the boiler of No. 46242 *City of Glasgow* from the frames and load it onto a 40 ton bogie flat trolley wagon for conveyance to Crewe works. *London Midland Region, BR*

Having dealt with the boiler, the frames are lifted off the driving wheels by the Willesden and Rugby cranes acting together to place them onto a wagon. *London Midland Region, BR*

addition a coach was cut up on the up electric platform, loaded onto wagons and taken away. To enable the tail of the crane to slew round during this loading operation, the colour light signal at the end of Platform 1 (down electric) and some overhead wires had to be temporarily removed and subsequently replaced.

Concurrently, work had also been proceeding on No. 46202. First the tender body, which had not been badly damaged and previously cleared of coal, was loaded on a bogie Rectank wagon, followed by the frame on another Rectank and dispatched by 8.15 am. At 10.50 am the task of lifting the large boiler was commenced and by 11.30 am it had been safely placed onto a 40 ton bogie Flatrol wagon. A temporary replacement bogie and pony truck were provided and the frames attached to the tender from No. 46257 in works grey by means of a long bulk timber coupling. Work went on throughout the Sunday loading up numerous parts which had either been knocked off at the time of the collision, or cut off later as part of the preparations carried out during the previous weeks, into further wagons, until ultimately a small trainload departed in the direction of Watford Jn at 9.30 pm behind LMS 4-6-0 'Black Five' No. 45282. The Rugby crane left at about the same time behind LMS 2-8-0 Stanier '8F' No. 48122, both engines having assisted throughout the operation along with No. 48601, another of the same type. The Willesden crane returned home at about 10.00 pm, after which all that remained of No. 46202 were the frames and the middle and rear sets of the driving wheels, the leading set having earlier been removed and put in a wagon. Thus the remains of *Princess Anne* departed on her own, or borrowed wheels in the early hours of Monday morning, 10th November towards Willesden at speed not exceeding 8 mph, while on the 13th November this assembly was seen heading north.

The electric lines were returned to traffic at the normal time early on Monday morning and the line in the siding, which had been obstructed since 8th October, brought into use again. Fortunately, the weather remained fine throughout weekend, thereby easing the task.

On Sunday, 16th November, a very similar operation was carried out on the other engine No. 46242 *City of Glasgow*. Towards the end of the main clearing up

With the debris cleared away and the up and down fast lines finally reopened to traffic, the restoration of platforms 2 and 3 remains to be completed, while platelayers fettle the track and a temporary scaffold footbridge is already in place. *Metropolitan Police Museum*

operation, this had been removed from the main line on Saturday 11th October, in a terrible condition and placed in a siding in the goods yard on the up side of the line at the Watford end. There was no need to interfere with ordinary traffic for this, as the cranes could use an adjacent track within the yard. To this end the necessary wagons were placed and the rest of the yard cleared on the Saturday afternoon in readiness for the work the next day. On Sunday morning the Willesden crane arrived to carry out a similar procedure, the boiler being removed and loaded on a bogie well trolley wagon Weltrol MK, with the main frames on a Rectank, a plate wagon, bogie bolster 'C' and a Flatrol were provided for other parts, while the wheels went into three open wagons. During the afternoon an engine arrived to take the train to North Wembley yard, where it was re-marshalled before heading off for Crewe. At the time, this engine appeared to be damaged much more than No. 46202, the frame being nothing but a twisted mass of scrap, whilst the smokebox had been forced right back, exposing all the tubes.

Sole Surviving Locomotive

The engine on the local train from Tring, No. 42389, sustained no damage as a result of the accident and indeed was used to tow away the undamaged coaches of the local train. It resumed working the same train within days and thereafter continued to work it regularly, a duty it shared with No. 42304 of the same 2-6-4T class.

At Crewe works Peter Rowledge, an engineering apprentice in the erecting shop at the time, recalls that it was a fine sunny morning when news began to filter through of a collision near London and further details were gleaned at lunch time from the radio news bulletin. Within a few weeks wreckage began to arrive in the works yard. The terrible damage suffered by No. 45637 meant that, apart from her boiler, she was withdrawn in December and scrapped without a second thought. By early January 1953, the frames of No. 46202 were in the erecting shop for assessment a little bent, while those of No. 46242 were beyond redemption and already awaiting scrapping.

The engine to the local train was of course at the remote end from the collision and was therefore able to continue in service without interruption. No. 42389 is seen here at Northampton Castle station on 30th May, 1959 hauling an Engineer's crane.

H.C. Casserley, courtesy J.A. Summerfield

No. 46202 had only recently emerged from Crewe works, following reconstruction from a steam turbine-propelled locomotive to one driven by conventional reciprocating motion at the cost of £8,875. Having since only run 11,443 miles, the authorities were loath to give up on her so lightly and she languished around the works for some time. In due course thoughts were given to the means of authorising a replacement, before eventually being withdrawn in May 1954, after which Rowledge recalls her remnants, minus boiler, stood for a long time on the scrap road in the 'melts', where engines were broken up. Even so, her boiler survived to join the pool of spares available for use on her sister engines. R.A. Riddles, Railway Executive Board member with responsibility for motive power matters, made her demise the excuse to obtain authority to built the single example of a British Railways Standard class '8P' Pacific locomotive, namely No. 71000 *Duke of Gloucester*, as the 11th locomotive in an order for 10 class '7' 'Britannias': Nos. 70045-54.

On the other hand, and perhaps surprisingly in view of its reported condition, following inspection by the works manager I.C. Forsyth and Frank Shaw, the chief erecting shop foreman, No. 46242 was gradually repaired and returned to traffic in October 1953 at a cost of £6,800. Its reconstruction may have utilised some original parts, but included new frames and resulted amongst other things in a revision to the front end of the platforms to the form of the originally un-streamlined engines. A spare boiler was always kept on hand for the 'Duchess' class, together with a full set of motion and cylinders and these were used to reconstruction the locomotive. Opportunity was also taken to fit a normal smokebox, rather than the tapered one all de-streamlined 'Coronation' Pacifics had until eventually replaced, as life expired, and to repaint her in BR green livery. Thus this engine became the only one of the three engines damaged in the accident to be repaired and restored to traffic. It survived until November 1963, by which time it had run over 1½ million miles.

No. 46242 *City of Glasgow* in reconstructed form was also allocated to royal duties as demonstrated by her arrival at platform 1 Euston on 8th July, 1958. Note the sweep of footplate from the buffer beam up over the cylinder. *M.S. Welch*

Chapter Seven

Official Responses

Coroner's Court

On 9th October, 1952 at the Church Hall, Wealdstone Dr A.P.L. Cogswell, the coroner for East Middlesex, sitting with a jury, opened the inquest on the 17 bodies of the victims held in the Wealdstone mortuary and then went on to the Hendon and Kilburn mortuaries. The Railway Executive was represented by S.P. Jones of its Legal Services, while J. Cleaver and Mr Holloway were in attendance on behalf of the Associated Society of Locomotive Engineers & Firemen (ASLEF) and the Union of Railway Signalmen (URS) respectively. The pathologists Keith Camps, Lee Hampton Pass and Donald Teare, on the basis of their post-mortem examinations, gave evidence on the cause of death. In all but one case, this was due to injuries sustained as a result of the accident, the one exception dying of heart failure brought on by shock. Particular attention was paid to driver Jones' health and it was asserted that he was perfectly healthy. The inquest was resumed at 2.00 pm on 30th October, 1952 and a verdict of accidental death passed in respect of all the victims.

The Ministry of Transport Inspector's Investigation

Lieutenant-Colonel G.R.S. Wilson, Railways Inspecting Officer to the Minister of Transport, having visited the site on the morning of the accident, opened the formal inquiry at 10.00 am on 15th October, 1952 at the Central Offices, Euston and resumed on 6th November. In his official report of 12th June, 1953 to the Minister he described the circumstances and factors leading up to the accident. It seemed obvious that, for whatever reason, the Perth train travelling on the up fast line had failed to heed the distant signal at caution, or to stop at either the outer and inner home signals protecting the local train from Tring, at the time about to depart from platform 4 of Harrow & Wealdstone station, it having just crossed from the up slow to the up fast line.

The question had to be, had Robert S. Jones, aged 43, the driver of the Perth train, and possibly Colin Turnock his fireman, missed the signals due to the foggy conditions, or were there other explanations? The Inspector went to considerable lengths to establish what the weather and other conditions locally actually were and whether the footplatemen on the Perth train had been seen and, if so, were they alert, by questioning the drivers of other trains that had recently passed, together with one of the fogmen going on duty.

On the day in question, patchy fog was widespread from Wigan southwards, through the Midlands and into North London, although later in the day it turned out to be fine, very warm, sunny and cloudless. Earlier in the morning the density of the fog at Harrow had been sufficient to warrant the implementation of the fog signalling procedure. On the other hand at the adjacent boxes of North Wembley and Hatch End neither signalman considered this necessary that morning, whereas at Bushey, where the up distant signals were of the semaphore type rather than the more usual colour light, the signalman did. The need for this was judged individually by the signalman and determined by whether he could clearly observe an agreed object at least 200 yards from his box. Instituting this procedure initially involved the length of the signal block section being extended by the adoption of double block working until such time as fogsignalmen were in place at the home and distant semaphore signals. Once in position, normal block working could be resumed. When the signal displayed stop, or caution, the fogsignalman would place detonators on the rails, which if passed by a train would explode, thereby giving a warning to the footplatemen. As this tied up permanent way staff in the unpleasant duty of acting as fogmen, there was naturally, therefore, a desire to revert to normal working as soon as the fog had cleared and in this case at Harrow fog working was lifted at 8.10 am, just nine minutes before the accident.

From the north end of Watford tunnel southward, the four tracks are straight through Watford Junction station, followed by a high embankment and viaduct on a right-handed curve, which continues nearly to Bushey. From here the line is straight through Bushey station, where the fourth rail electric lines join the main formation, followed by a long left-handed curve in a deep cutting where, during the days of steam engines, water troughs were situated to enable water to be picked up while the train was in motion. After these the line runs out of cutting onto embankment, and again a short length of straight in the run up to the Hatch End up colour light distant signals. At Hatch End station another long left-handed curve begins and continues on low bank followed by a shallow cutting for a short distance beyond the Harrow No. 1 colour light up distant signals, which were situated just north of a road overbridge close to Headstone Lane station. The four main steam lines are straight from then on to Harrow and for some distance beyond. From Tring all the way to Euston, apart from short rises north of Bushey and Primrose tunnel, the line is generally on a gradually falling gradient throughout.

The trains travelling towards London by this route that morning were as follows:

Summary of Up Trains

Train	10.20 pm ex-Glasgow	Mins late	8.15 pm ex-Perth	Mins late	7.31 am ex-Tring	Mins late
Engine	4-6-2 '8P'		4-6-2 '8P' No. 46242		2-6-4T No. 42389	
No. of coaches	14		11		9	
Crewe	4.18 am	40	4.37 am	32	-	-
Tring					7.31 am S	0
Watford Tunnel North End box	7.56 am F		8.01 to 8.03 am F		8.00 am S	
Watford Jn					8.06 am S	5
Hatch End	8.08 am F		8.17 am F		8.14 am S	
Harrow	8.11 am F	93	8.18 am F	80	8.17 am S	7

Note: F indicates that the train was travelling on the Fast line and S the Slow line.

It was found that the brakes of the Perth train had been applied at the very last moment, but they had not taken appreciable effect when its engine struck the rear of the local train at or about the top of the platform ramp, suggesting that the driver had only just realised the dire situation he was in. The combined train and locomotive's brake handle on the engine operated both the steam brake on the engine's coupled and tender wheels and the vacuum brakes on the coaches of the train. The calculated combined brake power was 69 per cent of the total weight of 525½ tons and all except one of the vehicles were fitted with direct admission valves which give a more rapid response of the train brakes to the driver's application. Even so, at this late stage, all was to no avail and the first collision had become inevitable.

A table of the distances at Harrow which are relevant to the primary collision between the Perth train and the local train is given below; the North and South references are to the actual point of collision at the country end of the up fast platform, and the lever numbers to those in Harrow No. 1 box:

Item	Lever No.	Direction	Distance (yards)
Up Fast and Up Slow **Distant signals**	45 & 37	**North**	**2,102**
Headstone Lane overbridge	-	North	2,079
Up Fast Outer Home	44	**North**	**628**
Up Slow directing Homes	36 & 38	North	333
Up Fast Inner Home	43	**North**	**188**
Trailing points of crossover			
Up Slow to Up Fast	18	North	80
Harrow No. 1 signal box	-	North	30
Point of first collision	-	-----	0
Harrow station footbridge No. 43	-	South	78
Front of engine of Perth train after collision	-	South	
Up Fast Starter	42	South	185
Up Fast Advanced Starter	41	South	694

Note: **Signals in bold type**, displaying Caution or Stop were all passed by Perth Express.

In assessing the conditions prevailing for trains travelling in the up direction, in addition to the local train and the express from Perth involved in the first collision, the Inspector gave consideration to the 10.20 pm express from Glasgow which had preceded the express from Perth on the same line all the way from Crewe. The driver of this train stated that, while travelling at a speed of between 55 and 60 mph, he had a clear view of the Harrow No. 1 up fast distant, at a distance of about 50 yards, a green and he asserted that he could not possibly have missed it.

Also, as they approached Harrow, both the local and the Perth trains had been passed by the 4.32 am down freight train from Norwood to Northampton, consisting of 58 empty wagons hauled by a heavy eight-coupled locomotive, travelling in the opposite direction on the slow line between Harrow and Hatch End a few minutes before the accident. Driver R.C. Brown and G.T. Lane, his fireman, stated that the visibility was about 200 yards, whilst the guard T. Starmer considered that by Headstone Lane it was a little less. The timing of this and the Perth train was such that it was just possible too that smoke from their locomotive drifted across the up fast colour light distant signal at the critical moment.

The local train had departed punctually from Tring, but gradually lost time due to the foggy conditions, and left Watford five minutes down. As planned it was due to cross from up slow to up fast at Harrow and the route through the crossover was set once the previous express from Glasgow on the up fast had cleared the section to North Wembley and the freight train on the down slow had passed. This crossover was subject to a speed restriction of 20 mph, so to ensure that the local train would not take this divergence too fast the signalman, although not required by the Regulations to do so for a booked diversion, held the up slow to up fast home signal at danger and only released it once the track circuit indicated that the local train was within 200 yards, thus ensuring that the driver had the speed of the local train under control.

On its way south the Perth express arrived at Crewe 13 minutes late and further time was lost in attaching engine No. 46242. The train left Crewe 19 minutes after the 10.20 pm express from Glasgow which had passed it while it was standing in the station. Although the Perth train was still losing time in the fog, it was nonetheless gradually catching up with the Glasgow train as they both journeyed south. Following several checks, once the Glasgow train had been slowed by a 15 mph temporary speed restriction through Watford tunnel, the Perth train was finally brought to a stop for two minutes by signals at the signal box to the north of the tunnel. It restarted at approximately 8.03 am, seven minutes after the Glasgow train had passed. At about this time, the local train had passed the North End box on the slow line and had stopped at Watford station from 8.04 to 8.06 am.

On setting off again, due to the speed restriction, the Perth train only gathered momentum slowly through the tunnel, but on emerging with all signals clear through Watford Jn, Bushey and Hatch End, speed was recovered rapidly with the powerful engine and the moderate load on the falling gradient. The recorded passing times made by the signalmen in their train registers suggested that it had covered the six miles from Watford to Harrow somewhat faster than the Glasgow train. By the time of the first collision, the Perth train was seven or eight minutes behind the Glasgow train and was approximately one hour and 20 minutes late.

The signal box immediately previous to Harrow was at Hatch End and directly the 'Train Out of Section' bell code from Harrow No. 1 for the Glasgow train on the up fast was received by the signalman, he offered the Perth train and it was accepted at once. In clear weather conditions the signalman at Harrow was fully entitled to admit the Perth train up to his outer home signal and still allow the local train to cross to the fast line ahead of it. But instead of stopping at the outer home the Perth train ran past this and the inner home without any apparent reduction in speed. It then burst through and damaged the trailing points of the up slow to up fast junction, which was still locked reversed with the up fast starting signal clear, and collided violently with the stationary local train. On seeing that the Perth train was not going to stop, the signalman in Harrow No. 1 box had placed a pair of detonators of the up fast, using the detonator placing machine immediately outside his box. As already mentioned there was evidence that at the last moment an emergency application of the vacuum brake had been made before the collision, but too late and to no avail.

The third train involved in this triple collision was the 8.00 am Liverpool and Manchester express from Euston. Owing to a minor vacuum brake defect, which was quickly rectified, its departure had been delayed by five minutes, but with two engines there was plenty of motive power and lost time was rapidly being regained. As the train approached Harrow with all signals clear at a speed of about 60 mph, these were thrown to danger by the signalman once he saw that a collision was imminent on the up fast line, but the train was already too close and a second collision was inevitable. The 'Obstruction Danger' bell signal was promptly sent to Hatch End and to North Wembley.

On Wednesday 8th October driver Jones was called at his house by the shedman at about 1.45 am and had booked on duty an hour later. The crew left Crewe North shed with No. 46242 at approximately 3.45 am. Engine movements and station working generally at Crewe were behindhand due to the fog, and the Perth train did not leave on its journey south until 4.37 am, 32 minutes late.

To establish whether sudden illness had caused driver Jones to miss the signals, a general post-mortem examination was undertaken by Dr Donald Teare. He reported that there was nothing to suggest that Jones was not a perfectly healthy man and that he was not suffering from the effects of diabetes, alcoholism or carbon monoxide poisoning at the time of the accident.

Once it was possible to reach the cab of the engine, railway officials and the coroner's officer crawled in. They found the regulator fully closed and the screw reverser in forward gear at 60 per cent cut off, which was the normal position for coasting, while the blower was open by one turn of the screw valve. Unless making up time, it was quite usual for drivers of up express trains, after taking water at Bushey, to close the regulator and coast all the way to Euston apart for a brief application of steam near Willesden. On the other hand, the driver's hand was on the vacuum brake valve handle in its fully applied position, hard over to the left, which suggested that Driver Jones had made no attempt to stop until the very last moment.

The Inspector reported that he was entirely satisfied that the first collision occurred due to driver Jones failing to heed the Harrow No. 1 up fast distant signal at caution and reduce the speed of the Perth train sufficiently to be able to stop at the up outer home signal, and that he subsequently passed the outer and inner homes at danger. He considered it probable that driver Jones made a last minute brake application just before the engine reached the detonators at the signal box, possibly when he caught sight of the inner home signal at danger, or he may by then have seen the obstruction ahead. He absolved signalman Armitage of all responsibility and considered that, once the first collision had taken place, nothing could have been done to prevent the down Liverpool/Manchester express from colliding at speed with the obstruction created.

As a result of the death of the two footplatemen, it was only possible to speculate on the circumstances of the human failure which led to the first collision. Driver Jones was an engineman of considerable experience and mature age with a good record. His handling of the train earlier in the journey from Crewe suggested that he had been driving in a professional manner in the fog. He had clearly been fully alert at Watford (North End) when he stopped for the signal and it did not appear that the conditions from there to the point of the accident were so poor that in daylight he should have lost his location. Bushey troughs are another unmistakable landmark, but, due to the damage to the tender, it was not possible to say whether water had been taken there, while by Hatch End the visibility had by 8.00 am improved to about 500 yards. Most regular travellers, such as commuters, can confirm that one soon becomes aware of the passing features, particularly changing sounds. These include passing over points and crossings; over and underbridges; the proximity of retaining walls; and a phenomenon known as 'roaring rails', each of which will have an individual signature. In ordinary circumstances, therefore, the approach to one's station, or in the driver's case signals, even in the dark, ought not to be a surprise.

From his quite recent experience of the route driver Jones should have known as he was passing Hatch End where he was and that the next signal would be the Harrow No. 1 up fast distant. In view of Dr Teare's report, his being temporarily incapacitated by the onset of sudden illness seemed highly improbable. Following a meticulous examination of the engine, no defect, which was considered might have distracted his attention, could be found. Likewise there was no evidence that a blow back had occurred through the fire hole door. In the circumstances the Inspector could only conclude that driver Jones had for some unexplained reason momentarily relaxed his concentration on the line ahead, at any rate for long enough at the speed he was going, perhaps in a deceptive patch of denser fog, to miss the colour light distant signal at eye level. If having missed the distant, he may have been surprised on reaching the Harrow semaphore stop signals, at a considerably higher elevation than the distant expected, and only braked when he caught sight of the inner home at danger or the local train in front of him.

When the cab of No. 46242 was examined, amongst all the damage, it was noted that, whilst the two water gauge glasses were intact, the drain pipe and cock of the left-hand water gauge had been torn away and must have released some steam and hot water into the cab. Despite the Inspector not picking up on the point, it has been suggested, by Stanley Hall in *Steam Railway* for September 2002, that this might have occurred prior to the collision and that the escaping steam might have resulted in a distraction at the critical moment, leading to driver Jones missing the crucial distant signal. Well, may be, but, if so, this must have happened in the four or five minutes since lengthman H.J. Richards, who having just reached his post at the distant signals at Bushey, recollected distinctly seeing a cloth waved from the left-hand side of the footplate in acknowledgement of his own wave of a hand to indicate that the up fast distant signal was clear as the Perth train passed him.

The late running of the three trains concerned only contributed to the accident in the sense that it happened to bring them into proximity at the same time and place. Had they been on time, then it might equally have been other trains. In the ordinary course of managing conflicting movements one of the two up trains had to be held at signals, so as to permit the other to proceed. In this the safety of railway traffic must at all times depend on the obedience to signals. The practice of giving precedence to the London residential trains in the morning over late running main line expresses, as in foggy weather, was defended. In order to keep residential trains as nearly as possible to time and avoid the dislocation of other movements, it was necessary to maintain their planned routes on the fast and slow lines at the expense of further delays to the long distance expresses, either at the junction crossover from slow to fast lines, or in the ordinary course of block working, as these merely affect the efficiency of traffic operation rather than safety.

The Inspector considered that patchy fog in the section may have contributed to the first collision. Nonetheless, the visibility at Harrow No. 1 box was appreciably more than the minimum required for normal working. Signalmen, however, acted under the guidance of arbitrary rules which cannot provide for every contingency. By virtue of the professional skill and care of engine drivers throughout the country in the performance of their duties, the Rules and Regulations for train working in fog had in practice proved adequate on the vast majority of occasions. He was of the opinion that the way to prevent the occasional case of human failure, such as that encountered at Harrow, did not lie in tightening up the regulations to the detriment of traffic movement, but in improving the drivers' vigilance by providing them with a positive link with the state of lineside signals. Warning systems afford valuable protection against failure of the driver to respond to a distant signal at caution. Experience had shown that if speed was not reduced when the distant signal was passed at caution there was a grave risk that subsequent stop signals would also be disregarded, which otherwise might lead to a collision or derailment on a turnout at high speed with very serious consequences.

Following the accident and rebuilding No. 46242 *City of Glasgow* was clearly in no way inferior to her sisters, as she was selected to haul the first down 'Caledonian' on 17th June, 1957. She is seen here at Euston station about to depart on the inaugural run with a pipe band and number of dignitaries in attendance. *M.S. Welch*

Chapter Eight

Automatic Warning System

The Government had been urging the railways for many years to give serious consideration to the extension of automatic train control (ATC), although in its eventual form it became known as the automatic warning system (AWS). In 1922 and again in 1927 the Government had set up special committees to review improved railway safety, under the chairmanship of Colonel Sir John Pringle, the Chief Inspecting Officer. In 1930 the report of the second of these recommended either direct (automatic) or indirect methods, with a general preference for the former as exemplified by the ATC system initiated by the Great Western Railway (GWR) in 1905 and by then in fairly extensive use on its network. Since the development of the GW contact system at the beginning of the 20th century, however, technology had advanced and the Pringle Committee recognised the potential advantages of the non-contact magnetic Hudd system and recommended that full scale prototype trials should be undertaken in working conditions.

Indirect methods considered included increasing the intensity and penetrative power of signal luminaires and the development of certain types of block control, designed to prevent errors by signalmen. Although the report was referred to the railway companies, in the economic constraints of the time, soon to be followed by the outbreak of World War II, none, except for the Great Western, considered that automatic train control could justify the cost of installation of equipment on trains and lineside plant, in view of the small number of accidents which were likely thereby to be avoided. Instead they indicated that indirect methods were preferred and should be further developed. Nonetheless, they did agree that further exploration of automatic train control should be pursued and pointed out that some trials with more modern apparatus were in progress.

They were referring to the fact that both the Southern and London Midland and Scottish railways had carried out preliminary trials with the Hudd system in 1931 and 1932. The latter took the process a step further when, in 1937, it installed the system on the London, Tilbury and Southend Section, equipping 150 locomotives for use on the 37 route miles between Fenchurch Street, Tilbury and Southend, this being finally approved by the Ministry after World War II in 1947. The LNER, following a serious collision at Castlecary (Scotland), when 35 were killed and 179 injured, also began in 1938 to install the same system between Edinburgh and Glasgow, but their work was brought to a halt by the outbreak of war the following year. The Great Western on the other hand continued to extend its contact system until most of its main lines were equipped. The Southern Railway, with its intense electric passenger services, preferred, instead, to place priority on the installation of continuous track circuiting, to operate multiple aspect colour light signalling, maintaining with some justification that the arresting effect of a succession of colour light signals rendered automatic train control less necessary. They further contended that track circuiting, particularly when forming part of substantial lengths of an automatic colour light signalling scheme, was a better means of preventing mistakes by signalmen, which could not be claimed for automatic train control.

The driver's disregard or misinterpretation of a colour light distant signal in daylight and clear weather at Bourne End, about 15 miles down the line from Harrow & Wealdstone, on 30th September, 1945, resulted in a serious accident, with the loss of 43 lives and 124 passengers injured, which again placed the subject in the spotlight. In his report of this accident, the then Chief Inspecting Officer, Lieutenant-Colonel Sir Alan Mount, strongly recommended the application of warning control to main lines, and in their response the railway companies were specifically requested to address this issue and other items when submitting their proposals on the recommendations of the report to the Minister. When they did so in December 1947, they naturally referred to the implications on scarce resources of skilled manpower and finance to undertake the general installation of automatic train control on main lines, particularly if not part of the modernisation of signalling. In the meantime another serious accident had occurred at Goswick on 26th October, 1947, when a semaphore distant was ignored at caution, leading to 28 fatalities and 65 hospitalised. As a consequence Sir Alan Mount in his Annual Report for 1947, concluded with a reference to automatic train control by saying that, 'there were substantial grounds for the extension of such equipment, and it deserves high priority in relation to other operating and signalling improvements, particularly as the majority of railway mileage is likely to remain signalled under the semaphore system for a long time'.

At the time of Nationalisation of the railway companies on 1st January, 1948, there were two systems of warning control in regular use. The older and by far the most extensive was the Great Western contact system which had been installed on 1,356 route miles. In this system as a locomotive approached a distant signal, a fixed insulated ramp in the space between the running rails, known as the 'four foot' in railway parlance, raised a plunger on the locomotive. If the distant signal was set at caution, no electrical current was supplied to the ramp and the raising of the plunger actuated a siren in the cab and made a light application of the brake which the driver could then cancel. On the other hand, with the distant signal displaying clear, a small electric current was supplied to the ramp and hence to the engine, preventing the siren and brake from acting and instead resulted in the sounding of a bell in the cab.

The more recent system developed by A.E. Hudd, as modified by the London Midland and Scottish Railway, was in use on only 37 route miles between Bow and Shoeburyness on their London, Tilbury and Southend Section, a line running on the north bank of the estuary of the River Thames and notorious for fogs. It eliminated the need for physical contact, by relying on the effect of magnetism. A permanent magnet, followed at a short distance by an electrically operated magnet, was again located in the 'four foot' at the distant signal. If the distant signal was at caution, the electromagnet remained un-energised, so when the permanent magnet attracted the armature of a receiver mounted under the locomotive, its reversal opened a small valve and thereby reduced the vacuum in a pilot reservoir. This in turn actuated a long blast on a small siren and provided a cancellable brake application, in the same manner as the Great

Western system. When the distant signal was displaying clear, a current to the electromagnet had the opposite polarity to the permanent magnet. The consequence of this was that the siren sounded only briefly as the permanent magnet was passed, because the receiver armature was quickly restored to normal by the electromagnet and before the brake could take effect. The audible signals on the footplate were clearly not so distinctive as the siren and bell of the Great Western system. The Hudd equipment was operated pneumatically, there being no electric circuits on the locomotive.

The Railway Executive then gave their consideration to the merits of the two systems. At first they were inclined to favour the Great Western contact system, but there proved to be technical objections to the use of this in electrified areas due to the risk of stray currents from the traction feed adversely affecting the AWS. Although the Hudd system embodied the non-contact principle which was desirable, it was not considered wholly satisfactory, mainly because the lack of sufficient differentiation between the caution and clear indications. In 1951 the Railway Executive decided to develop the apparatus combining the best features of both systems, utilising electrical operation on the engine. Preliminary trials were carried out between London Marylebone and Neasden and development work on the East Coast main line between New Barnet and Huntingdon, later extended over a total of 105 miles to Grantham. Due to various practical difficulties, trials did not get into full swing until December 1950, when 54 engines had been fitted with a modified apparatus and these trials continued during 1951.

Difficulties continued to occur, however, with wrong side failures and it was August 1952 before these were resolved and drawings for the final prototype design were completed. Before a locomotive fitted with the equipment was ready on 17th October, 1952, however, the terrible accident at Harrow had occurred. A satisfactory conclusion to the trials and the implementation of the system now became top priority.

In its developed form the track equipment consisted of a pair of magnets situated approximately 200 yards on the approach side of each semaphore distant, rather than stop signals, and multi-aspect colour light signal. The first is a permanent magnet followed within 2 feet 6 inches by an electromagnet. If a semaphore distant is clear or a multi-aspect signal is displaying green, a bell rings in the cab for two to four seconds, while when a semaphore distant is at caution or a multi-aspect colour light is at red, yellow or double yellow, the siren sounds and a brake application is commenced. The driver can cancel the siren and brake as proof that he is alert, but any attempt to anticipate the warning by premature operation of the cancelling handle only results in a brake application. Following the use of the cancelling handle a visual indication is displayed in front of the driver, and remains there until reset to normal as the engine passes the next set of track apparatus.

The Minister of Transport & Civil Aviation had been involved in approving various stages throughout and finally sanctioned adoption of the developed system for use on vacuum braked trains on 30th November, 1956. Once the Chief Inspecting Officer was completely satisfied with the efficiency and reliability of the system, the British Transport Commission announced that they were prepared authorise a five-year plan at an estimated cost of £7.5 millions, and a long term plan which, including the five-year plan, would bring the estimated total capital cost to £17.3 millions with corresponding annual charges estimated at between £1 million and £2 millions.

Work on installation of the five-year plan, which covered 1,332 route miles route over the lines from Euston to Glasgow, King's Cross to Edinburgh, Edinburgh to Glasgow, Euston to Birmingham, Manchester and Liverpool, Liverpool Street to Norwich and Waterloo to Exeter, Southampton and Bournemouth, did not begin until 1958 and the system only came into use on significant lengths from 1960. This, unfortunately, was not before further accidents with loss of life, which might have been prevented by AWS, had occurred at Welwyn Garden City on 7th January, 1957 with one death and 25 injured, five seriously; St Johns, Lewisham when in fog again 90 were killed and 109 injured on 4th December, 1957; and on 31st January, 1958 when in foggy conditions 10 lost their lives and 89 were injured at Dagenham East. The long term plan was intended to cover an additional 3,988 route miles, giving a total of 5,320 route miles (plus the 1,393 route miles already equipped pre-Nationalisation). The Hudd system on the London, Tilbury and Southend section was converted to the BR standard system in 1962. By 1988, just over 7,300 route miles were fitted with BR AWS; all the former GWR equipment had been replaced by the BR system.

The automatic warning system is essentially a cautionary device to aid drivers observing the signals, rather than an absolute train stop system. In this form it served the railways well until, with the advent of much faster trains, the accidents at Southall on 19th September, 1997 and at Ladbroke Grove on 5th October, 1999 led to the call for a more sophisticated system of regulating the speed of approaching trains and ensuring that signals are not passed at danger. As required by the Railway Safety Regulations of 1999, this need is currently being met by the installation of the train protection and warning system (TPWS) throughout Network Rail's network over all lines that carry passengers at a cost of £500 million. A series of censor loops, looking like a miniature garden gate, in the 'four foot' of the track are being fitted in rear of 11,000 signals, 700 buffer stops and 2,700 permanent speed restrictions. The first loop passed initiates a timer on the train, so that if the train passes a second trigger loop within one second, both some distance in advance of the signal, the brakes are automatically applied. By this means a train travelling at 70 mph (115 kph) will be brought to a stand within the 'safe overrun distance', usually 200 yards (185m) beyond the signal, and trains travelling at greater speed will have their velocity significantly reduced.

Chapter Nine

Conclusions

The magnitude of the task facing the professional railwaymen, medical teams and emergency services, together with the volunteers undertaking the recovery of the dead and injured, followed by the clearing of the wreckage and restoration of the railway infrastructure, cannot be over estimated. The size of the double collision resulted in the very substantial toll of those killed and injured and a heap of wreckage was enough to swamp many an organisation. To work flat out so desperately, with little respite for so long, is both physically and mentally exhausting, leaving those involved so fatigued that their performance dropped dramatically, leading to the need to find fresh resources from outside the immediate area. That the London Midland Region, with the assistance of its neighbours, managed to reopen all lines within five days, speaks volumes of the dedication of those that laboured so hard that week.

Nonetheless, the manner in which emergency procedures operated, was in most cases reviewed. For instance, because the Metropolitan Police were on site in significant numbers at an early stage, it was their senior officers who controlled operations, set up and organised the rescue squads, whereas the Fire Service had equal responsibility and in the end it was for the railway to manage the rescue and undertaking to clear up the debris to enable the lines to be opened again for traffic. Likewise, it took some time for sufficient railway police to assemble from distant locations, to be able to protect the site within railway property and in the meantime the security function was fulfilled by the Met.

Following the accident, there seems to have been some heart searching as to who should actually be in charge at a scene such as this. Alf Wooder CBE, the Chief Fire Officer of the Middlesex Fire and Ambulance Service, together with Mr Dennis their solicitor, were so concerned that they summoned a meeting with senior officers of the Metropolitan Police on 16th October, 1952 to discuss the issue. While there was a risk of fire, the former contended that under the Fire Services Act 1947 the senior fire officer was solely responsible until the fire was extinguished, but thereafter their duty ceased. Nonetheless, they had remained on the scene for more than 3½ days, clearing debris and assisting with the rescue of the injured and removal of the dead, yet they were under no obligation to deal with rescue operations. The Met. agreed that once the fire brigade had arrived, the duty of the police was to keep people back so as not to hamper operations. The responsibility in this case was really one for the Railway Police, but prior to their arrival it was right and proper for the civil police to take charge from the police angle and only remain at the request of the railway authorities. Informing the relatives of casualties and of crowd control on the public highway was a matter for the civil police.

So, when J.W. Watkins, the Chief Regional Officer of the London Midland Region of British Railways with six of his senior staff met with senior officers of the Metropolitan Police and Middlesex Fire and Ambulance Service, on 13th November, 1952 to review how matters had gone, discussion seems to have centred on who should be in overall charge at the scene at various stages following such an accident. BR stated that it was their Chief Operating Officer's responsibility to clear the debris. Perhaps unusually in this case senior officers had happened to be on one of the trains, but ordinarily the civil police forces were likely to arrive on the scene in any numbers first. BR were happy for them to be in charge until such time as their own police were able to get to the scene and would not hesitate to seek assistance from the civil police. Following the accident, Mr R. Richards, Chief Officer of British Transport Police had drawn up a draft memorandum for circulation to the County Police Forces endeavouring to clarify the situation for the future and, while the Metropolitan Police concurred with much, they still had a few reservations. Following the meeting, the delegates were entertained to lunch at the Euston Hotel.

Mr Wooder, reported to his Council on 16th October, 1952, discussing how the incident had been handled. He seems to be at pains to demonstrate that the management of the fire and ambulance resources was entirely satisfactory and what a good job he was performing. While he praises his staff's efforts and lists the tributes he received, he totally fails to question whether the work his men were expected to carry out was the best that could be achieved. For instance, apart from the casual mention of the provision of two ambulances from the American armed forces, quite incredibly he does not appear to recognise the important contribution made by the United States Air Force medical personnel.

It must have been obvious to most people that we had much to learn from the manner in which the Americans, with their experience of battlefield medicine in stabilising casualties (particularly the use of intravenous fluid in the form of blood plasma), before moving them for treatment, had responded to the crisis. At that time the ambulance service was usually part of the fire service and in London came under the control of nine different local authorities. There was no overall plan on how to cope with an accident of any size and only limited medical equipment was carried. Ambulance men were very much considered an adjunct to the fire service. With merely a first aid certificate from the British Red Cross or St John's Ambulance Brigade, they were considered to be drivers whose job was to 'scoop up and run' with the injured to the nearest hospital as quickly as possible. Likewise those doctors called to the scene were general practitioners totally unprepared to cope with the carnage confronting them. For instance, having administered pethadine, Dr Joseph Lister had to use a sticking plaster upon which to write, for the advice of the hospital, that the person had received the dose. Neither had they been given any formal medical training in how to bring treatment to the injured, prioritise victims and stabilise them on the scene, prior to removing them to hospital in an orderly fashion.

A major cause of confusion in the early hours was the indiscriminate filling of ambulances left unattended while crews worked on their own quota of allocated casualties. Not only were these ambulances full of casualties, but also empty of equipment! This resulted in the dispatch of a number of the more serious cases being delayed while less urgent cases were either conveyed to hospital or disembarked from the ambulances. Generally the provision of ambulances was not under the control of the local health board until 1959. Although the inadequacy of emergency medicine was noted in the medical press at the time of the accident, surprisingly it was to take another 20 years of slow development in the extent of training for ambulance staff before paramedics, as we know them today, arrived on the scene to minimise the loss of lives once the accident had occurred, particularly during the first crucial hour.

In the late 1960s the London Emergency Services Liaison Panel was founded comprising representatives of the Metropolitan and City of London Police, London Fire Brigade, London Ambulance Service, St John's Ambulance, local authority borough and county emergency planners and various co-opted members. At their monthly meetings recent incidents were reviewed, new or revised procedures drafted; arrangements made for new communication equipment to be tested and reported upon; inter-service exercises organised and critically assessed. Nonetheless, it was to take another 10 years of slow development to formulate and persuade politicians to support their recommendations for the implementation of a proper National Major Emergency Plan for major incidents, such as civil riots; railway and aeroplane accidents; explosions; and sieges, major in this context being defined as one in which there were more than 50 casualties.

The St John's Ambulance Brigade was likewise keen to learn from the experience and their Major H.C. Stewart organised a Surgeons' Conference on 15th March, 1953 at their premises in Collingham Gardens, Earls Court. As well as their own representatives, this was attended by J. White, Assistant Chief Inspector of the Metropolitan Police; D.D. Ivall, Deputy Chief Officer of the Middlesex Fire & Ambulance Service; Lt Col G.P. Wiedeman, Deputy Chief Surgeon, 3rd Air Force, USAF; L.W. Cox, Deputy Operating Superintendent and Dr G.E. Graves Pierce, Regional Medical Officer, both of London Midland Region, BR. It was concluded that the Brigade could have been of greater assistance had it been possible in an emergency to contact their personnel more quickly and if their staff in mufti could be more readily identified on the scene to the public services and their own members. Again the North West Regional Hospital Board met on the afternoon of 19th November at 13 Portland Place to discuss the ramifications of the incident.

On the railway one assumes similar reviews of their procedures were undertaken. It has been suggested that the huge task of mounting the rescue operation, managing the disruption to railway operations and clearing up the aftermath strained the railway organisation to the limit. Whether previously envisaged in cases of emergency or not, as those first on site tired with no end in sight to their mammoth task, it is clear that manpower and resources had to be drafted in from far and wide, including staff from neighbouring Regions of British Railways and London Underground Railways. One consequence was that on 26th June, 1953 the Railway Executive's Motive Power Committee appointed an 'ad hoc' committee to report on the arrangements for breakdown trains and cranes. They submitted their report in 1955 and this eventually led to the acquisition of 12 new 75 ton and 10 further 30 ton breakdown cranes and the provision of new updated breakdown riding/mess and tool vans to a standardised layout, so that relief crews from other areas would know where to find equipment.

The terrible consequences of passing signals at danger can have left no one in any doubt that some form of automatic warning system was an absolute necessity for lines carrying passenger trains. These had been under development for many years and had reached an advanced stage by the time of the accident, but it was to be a few more years yet before installation of such a system began to be undertaken on any substantial length of the national network.

No practicable form of carriage construction can be guaranteed to prevent casualties when heavy trains collide at high speed, as the energy which has to be dissipated in a short time and/or the space, where available, necessary to reduce momentum is substantial. The few, then recently introduced, new BR Mark I stock standard coaches were randomly marshalled fourth, sixth and eleventh in the Liverpool/Manchester train. Had a higher proportion of the rolling stock been of the latest all-steel type more rigidly coupled together, the wreckage at Harrow might have been less compact and the fatalities and other casualties thereby reduced. At the time, however, ordinary screw couplings were normal on the trains of the former London Midland and Scottish and Great Western railways. For economic reasons railway coaches were, and still are, built to be long lasting, and many years were to elapse before the standard coaches predominated, even in long distance trains. This led to there being a long transition period before buckeye couplings came into general use with corridor stock on these routes.

Postscript

Christ Church, St Alban's Road in North Watford, was attended by many railwaymen and their families living in the vicinity. They would, therefore, have been familiar with the East window of the church put in during 1935 in memory of Charlotte Elizabeth Wells and Ralph Edward Thorpe. After the railway accident, the whole sanctuary of the church was remodelled as a memorial to all 112 who died on the morning of 8th October, 1952. To mark this, the central panel of the East window was altered in 1953 to include a memorial plaque at its foot. In addition, and at the same time, a memorial to the Watford victims was mounted on the West wall of the church.

In 1997 a stainless steel memorial plaque was attached to the side of the ramp on the approach to the public library adjacent to the Civic Centre, reading as follows:

> LONDON BOROUGH OF HARROW
> In memory of the 112 people who lost their lives
> in the Wealdstone rail crash on 8th October 1952.
> Unveiled on 8th October 1997, the 45th anniversary of
> Britain's worst peacetime rail disaster
> by The Mayor of Harrow, Councillor Keith Toms.

In Memoriam

Robert J. Austin	Wealdstone	Edwin M. Mocaon	Birmingham
John M. Beattie	Glasgow	James M. Muir	Vantage House, Fife
Ernest A. Benjafield	Edmonton	Peter Mullins	Pinner
D. Bentin	Walsall, Staffs	George Munroe	Perth
Clifford M. Bentley	Walsall, Staffs	Francis W. Murray	Kenton
H.G. Blake	Kenton	William K. Nash	Watford
Horace Blundell	Stanmore	Allan W. Neale	Stanmore
Leonard Blundell	Harrow	Arthur V. Nelson	New Ferry, Cheshire
E.G. Briers	Watford	John W. Newlyn	Walworth, SE17
Herbert N. Brooks	Watford	Peter Parker	Wealdstone
Walter F. Burgess	Wealdstone	Peter Parkinson	Wealdstone
Charles H. Burton	Hendon	Betty I. Paskins	Wealdstone
Henry Burton	Kensington, W8	Albert Perkins	Liverpool
Polly Burton, Mrs	Michigan, USA	Peter Philpot	Harrow
G. Cheetham, Mrs	Wigan	Leslie Pine	Watford
George M. Christopher	Watford	John G. Pitman	Stanmore
J.W. Chubb, Mr	Tring	A.W. Poultney	Stanmore
C.G.F. Clark	Hatch End	David E. Pratt	Watford
George Clark	Watford	Leslie Preston	Bushey
E.M. Clough, Mr	Harrow	Mary Proctor	Briarfield, Lancs
Fredrick Colbourn	Stanmore	George Quayle	Askam-in-Furness, Lancs
R.D. Cole, Mr	Stanmore	Alice A. Raward	Harrow
Ronald C. Cosier	Tring	W. Reid	Kirkcaldy, Fife
J.W. Crocker, Mr	Watford	Ernest M. Ridgeway	Watford
Valerie A. Cross	Watford	Joseph Riley	South Shields
John N. Crow	Stanmore	Clara Robinson	Wigan
Raymond H. Culverhouse	Watford	John Robinson	Radipole, Dorset
Henry W. Derbyshire	Watford	A.J. Rodwell	Watford
Ronald N. Dobson	Knaresborough, Yorks	Charles Roff	Watford
Bartholomew Doherty	Watford	John E. Rodgers	Watford
Nora L. Edge	Watford	Stanley J. Russell	Watford
Geoffrey D. Ellington	Ramsey, Hunts	Margaret A. Sabin	Watford
William F. Emery	Watford	William G. Safe	Salisbury, Wilts
Sydney Farrington	Stanmore	John Schofield	Chadwell Heath
John Glover	Hemel Hempstead	Norman Shelton	Whittlesea, Cambs
L.F. Grant, Mr	Bermondsey, SE1	John L. Shepherd	Billingham, C Durham
F. Hardcastle, Mr	Kenton	Donald G. Sheppard	Wembley Park
Allan Hargreaves	Bolton	Maurice H. Sifton	Harrow Weald
John W. Hardy	Lancaster	Adam G.W. Slack	Penrith, Cumberland
Louise Hardy	Lancaster	Gordon W. Slater	Derby
Ann Heard	Croxley Green	Jean Smith	Watford
M.H. Hilton, Mr	Watford	B.M. Stretch	Watford
George E. Holland	Camberwell	Agnes Swaine	Michigan, USA
Peter Hopkinson	Hemel Hempstead	Francis C. Taverner	Berkhamsted
William Howard	Watford	Kathleen G. Taylor	Watford
H.J. Jefferson	Kenton	Harry G. Tebbenham	West Wickham, Kent
Robert S. Jones	Crewe	Natalie Turner	Kings Langley
Audrey Keating	Watford	Colin Turnock	Wistaston, Cheshire
Thomas Kelly	Liverpool	Hilda M Walter, Mrs	Harrow
James W. Kemster	Tunbridge Wells, Kent	R.T. Watson	Stanmore
James Kenyon	Sunderland	W.E. Webster	Stanmore
Edith E. Law	Tadworth, Surrey	Norman H. Whitehead	Berkhamsted
Rosetta Lawrence	Slough	Trevor H. Whitfield	Hemel Hempstead
William Ledger	Hatch End	Herbert Williams	Mill Hill East, Finchley
John M. Masters	Westerham	Donald G. Woodall	HQ 59 Maintenance Group, 124 USAF
A. Meacham	Watford	May J. Woodall	HQ 59 Maintenance Group, 124 USAF

Left: The memorial stone sited on the external face of Harrow & Wealdstone station, photographed on 6th July, 2003. The engraved lettering is not highlighted. It reads, 'IN MEMORY OF THE 112 PEOPLE WHO LOST THEIR LIVES AT HARROW AND WEALDSTONE ON OCTOBER 8 1952'.

Edmund A. Stanbrook

Over the past five years since there was a campaign, led by local councillor Keith Toms and supported by the *Harrow Observer* newspaper, to have a more suitable memorial placed at the station in time to commemorate the 50th anniversary. This reached fruition in 2002, when Railtrack and Silver Link agreed that a proper memorial might be placed on the station.

Survivors, relatives and friends of the 112 people who were victims of the disaster, together with those injured or who had a hand in the recovery operation gathered on Sunday 6th October, 2002 at Christchurch in St Albans Road, Watford to remember before God their loved ones and the suffering which followed the accident. The following Tuesday 8th October, the actual 50th anniversary, a memorial plaque on the wall at the Eastern entrance to Harrow & Wealdstone station was unveiled by the Mayor John Branch. At 8.00 pm that same evening, a memorial service was held at Holy Trinity Church in Headstone Lane, attended by the Bishop of Willesden.

Harrow & Wealdstone station on 6th July, 2003. The stone memorial plaque sited below the Underground and British Rail signs is arrowed. *Edmund A. Stanbrook*

Appendix One

Composition of the Trains

7.31 am Tring to Euston Local Train

Item	No.	Origin	Diagram	Built	Description	Weight t. - cwt	Notes	Wdn
Loco.	42389	LMS	ED172B	1933	2-6-4T Fowler	86-5	a	
1st coach	M20823M	LMS	D1964	1936	BT	28-0	b	
2nd coach	M12005M	LMS	D1906A	1937	T	30-0	b	
3rd coach	M11780M	LMS	D1906A	1936	T	29-12	b	
4th coach	M11550M	LMS	D1784	1932	T	28-0	b	
5th coach	M11129M	LMS	D1700	1928	T	27-0	c	
6th coach	M11254M	LMS	D1700	1929	T	26-0	d	12/52
7th coach	M21183M	BR/LMR	D1964A	1952	BT	28-0	e	1/53
8th coach	M15202M	L&Y	D98	1921	T	26-0	e	11/52
9th coach	M14281M	MR	D1058	1920	T	24-0	e	11/52
Total weight of coaches						246-12		
Weight of locomotive						86-5		
Total weight of train						332-17		

8.15 pm Express Sleeper Perth to Euston

Item	No.	Origin	Diagram	Built	Description	Weight t. - cwt	Notes	Wdn
Loco.	46242	LMS	ED261C	1940	4-6-2 'Duchess'	161-12	f	
1st coach	W2931W	GW	O33	1940	Siphon G	25-16	e	11/52
2nd coach	M30432M	LMS	D1778	1925	BG	23-12	e, g	11/52
3rd coach	M1799M	LMS	D1899	1934	TK	31-17	e	11/52
4th coach	M26896M	BR/LMR	D2161	1950	BTK	30-0	e	1/53
5th coach	M4469M	LMS	D2117	1947	CK	31-0	e	11/52
6th coach	M1517M	LMS	D1860	1933	TK	30-17	h	
7th coach	M723M	LMS	D1947	1936	SLC	43-0	i	
8th coach	Sc706M	LMS	D1844	1931	SLC	42-0	i	
9th coach	M589M	LMS	D1863	1933	SLT	37-0	i	
10th coach	M370M	LMS	D1926	1936	SLF	41-16	i	
11th coach	M31086M	LMS	D2007	1940	BG	27-0	i	
Total weight of coaches						363-18		
Weight of locomotive & tender						161-12		
Total weight of train						525-10		

Notes

a. Undamaged.
b. Largely undamaged and subsequently towed away by No. 42389.
c. Later drawn away.
d. Bogie derailed, later drawn away.
e. Damaged beyond repair.
f. Severely damaged, but repaired.
g. No. M30432M originally recorded as M30437M. Error noted and corrected in June 1959.
h. Derailed and slightly damaged.
i. Largely undamaged and subsequently towed away.

Vehicle Codes

Code	Description
BG	Passenger full brake with gangway
BT	Third class non-corridor brake
BTK	Third class corridor brake
CK	Composite corridor
SLC	Composite sleeping car
SLF	First class sleeping car
SLT	Third class sleeping car
T	Third class non-corridor
TK	Third class corridor
Siphon G	Milk van with gangway

APPENDIX

8.00 am Express Euston to Liverpool & Manchester

Item	No.	Origin	Diagram	Built	Description	Weight t. - cwt	Notes	Wdn
1st Loco.	45637	LMS	176J	1934	4-6-0 'Jubilee'	133-4	a	12/52
2nd Loco.	46202	LMS	179?	35/52	4-6-2 rebuilt 'Turbomotive'	159-17	a	5/54
1st coach	M26856M	BR/LMR	D2161	1950	BTK	30-0	a	1/53
2nd coach	M4813M	LMS	D2117	1947	CK	31-0	a	1/53
3rd coach	M1124M	BR/LMR	D2162	1950	FK	30-0	a	1/53
4th coach	M34108	BR	181	1951	BTK	34-0	b	1/53
5th coach	M24683M	BR/LMR	D2159	1950	CK	29-17	a	1/53
6th coach	M34287	BR	181	1952	BTK	34-0	a	1/53
7th coach	M27266M	LMS	D1999	1946	RTO	30-0	a	1/53
8th coach	M30049	LMS	D1697	1926	RK	30-0	a	1/53
9th coach	M7465M	BR/LMR	D2160	1949	RFO	31-0	c	
10th coach	M1117M	BR/LMR	D2162	1950	FK	30-0	d	
11th coach	M34024	BR	181	1951	BTK	34-0	d	
12th coach	M30405M	LMS	D1778	1925	BG	23-12	d	
13th coach	M30947M	LMS	D1796?	1926	BG	24-0	d	
14th coach	E70148E	LNER	111	1928	BG	26-15	d	
15th coach	M31755M	LMS	D2130	1928	BG	26-0	d	
Total weight of coaches						444-4		
Weight of locomotives						293-1		
Total weight of train						737-5		

Notes
a. Damaged beyond repair.
b. Severely damaged.
c. Bogie derailed
d. No significant structural damage to underframes, later towed away.

Vehicle Codes

Code	Description
BG	Passenger full brake with gangway
BTK	Third class corridor brake
CK	Composite corridor
FK	First class corridor
RFO	First class vestibule dining coach
RK	Kitchen only car
RTO	Third class vestibule dining coach

Appendix Two

Train Diversions

Up Passenger Trains Diverted to St Pancras on 8th and 8th/9th October, 1952

Origin	Departure Time	Due at Euston	Route	Title/Remarks
Northampton	8.45 am	10.00 am	Wellingbro'	
Wolverhampton	6.40 am	10.05 am	Mkt Harbro'	
Wolverhampton	7.50 am	10.40 am	Mkt Harbro'	
Crewe	7.50 am	11.17 am	Nuneaton	
Northampton	10.00 am	11.27 am	Wellingbro'	
Heysham (boat train)	6.30 am	11.35 am	Nuneaton	The Ulster Express
Manchester	8.20 am	12.55 pm	Nuneaton	
Manchester	10.05 am	1.55 pm	Nuneaton	
Blackpool Central	10.00 am	3.20 pm	Nuneaton	
Llandudno	9.10 am	3.43 pm	Nuneaton	
Manchester	12.05 pm	3.51 pm	Nuneaton	
Liverpool	2.00 pm	5.45 pm	Nuneaton	
Glasgow	10.00 am	6.00 pm	Nuneaton	The Royal Scot
Manchester	2.20 pm	6.12 pm	Nuneaton	
Bangor	12.45 pm	6.28 pm	Nuneaton	
Perth	8.55 am	7.24 pm	Nuneaton	
Manchester	5.50 pm	9.25 pm	Nuneaton	The Comet, minus Colne portion
Glasgow	1.30 pm	10.00 pm	Nuneaton	The Midday Scot
Blackpool	5.05 pm	11.06 pm	Nuneaton	
Glasgow	9.25 pm	7.00 am (Th)	Nuneaton	Additional stops at Mkt Harbro' and Nuneaton
Perth	8.15 pm	7.20 am (Th)	Nuneaton	

Down Passenger Trains Diverted to Midland Line on 8th and 8th/9th October, 1952

Destination	Origin	Due from Euston	Title/Remarks
Manchester	Euston	8.30 am	
Manchester	Euston	9.45 am	The Comet
Glasgow	Euston	10.00 am	The Royal Scot
Carlisle and Blackpool	Euston	10.40/10.50 am	Combined train
Manchester	Euston	11.45 am	
Liverpool	Euston	12.30 pm	The Red Rose
Glasgow	St Pancras at 1.30 pm	1.15 pm	The Midday Scot
Liverpool	Euston	2.30 pm	
Manchester	St Pancras at 2.45 pm	2.45 pm	
Liverpool	St Pancras	3.45 pm?	
Manchester	Euston	3.45 pm	
Heysham	St Pancras	4.55 pm	The Ulster Express
Preston	Euston	6.20 pm	
Inverness and Perth	Euston	7.20/7.30 pm	Combined train
Aberdeen	Euston	8.30 pm	Turned at Cricklewood
Holyhead	Euston	8.50 pm	Irish Mail
Glasgow	St Pancras at 9.30 pm	9.10 pm	
Glasgow	Euston	9.25 pm	
Perth	Euston	10.52 pm	
Windermere	Euston	11.05 pm	
Glasgow	Euston	11.40 pm	
Crewe	Euston	12.02 am (Th)	Via Wellingbro' and Northampton
Manchester	Euston	12.20 am (Th)	
Liverpool	Euston	12.30 am (Th)	

Note: Trains from Euston travelled via Acton Wells, the Midland Main Line and Nuneaton.

Passenger Trains Diverted to and from Paddington

Origin	Departure time	Route inwards	Returned at	Routes outwards	Title/Remarks
Blackpool and Holyhead	8.00 am	Market Drayton, Wolverhampton LL	5.50 pm (5.05/5.15 pm)	Bushbury Jn and Stafford	15 coach combined/ divided at Crewe
Liverpool	8.10 am	Nuneaton and Leamington	5.00 pm (4.30 pm)	Bushbury Jn and Stafford	15 coaches
Carlisle	8.20 am	Market Drayton	-	Kensington	Empty to Willesden
Wolverhampton	9.45 am	Birmingham and Leamington	6.08 pm (5.45 pm)	Bushbury Jn	The Midlander 10 coaches
Manchester	9.45 am	Market Drayton	6.23 pm (6.00 pm)	Bushbury Jn and Stafford	The Mancunian 12 coaches
Liverpool	10.10 am	Market Drayton	7.12 pm (6.07 pm)	Bushbury Jn and Stafford	The Merseyside 15 coaches
Wolverhampton	11.55 am	Leamington	-	Kensington	Empty to Willesden
Manchester	4.05 pm	Nuneaton and Leamington	-	Kensington	Empty to Willesden
Liverpool	4.10 pm	Rugby and Leamington	8.45 am (9/10)	Bushbury Jn and Stafford	13 coaches
Manchester	-	-	10.45 pm	Bushbury Jn	Van train
Liverpool	5.25 pm	Market Drayton	12.30 pm (9/10)	Bushbury Jn and Stafford	The Red Rose

Note: All departures called at Leamington Spa, Bimingham and Wolverhampton.
Times shown in brackets indicate the original scheduled time of departure from Euston.

Trains terminated at and despatched from other stations

Origin	Departure Time	Terminated at/ Started from	Returned as (ex-Euston)	Destination and Remarks
-	-	Watford Jn	12.00 noon	Crewe
-	-	Watford Jn	3.05 pm	Rugby
Wolverhampton	4.05 pm	Watford Jn	7.15 pm	Northampton and extended to Wolverhampton
-	-	Watford Jn	7.40 pm	Stranraer with sleepers at 10.20 pm
Birmingham	7.40 pm	Watford Jn	9.35 pm	Birmingham 6 coaches at 11.15 pm
Manchester	10.33 pm	Marylebone	-	Via Bletchley
-	-	Maiden Lane	1.37 am (Th)	Wolverhampton
-	-	Marylebone	2.15 am (Th)	Northampton via Calvert

Freight Trains Diverted on 8th/9th October, 1952

Down Trains

Depart	Origin	Destination	Route
6.00 pm	Camden	Carlisle	Wakefield
9.30 pm	Camden	Crewe	Acton and Western Region
10.30 pm	Camden	Copley Hill, Leeds	Canonbury (GN) and Wakefield
11.06 pm	Camden	Stockport	Canonbury (GN), Colwick and Egginton (GN)
12.30 am (Th)	Camden	Carlisle and Glasgow	Canonbury (GN), Wakefield and Hellifield
1.00 am (Th)	Camden	Birmingham	Canonbury (GN), Peterborough & Rugby
2.00 am (Th)	Camden	Crewe	Acton and Western Region

Up Trains

3.50 pm	Carlisle	Broad Street	Midland Main Line (meat train)
7.52 pm	Bushbury	Camden	Luffenham and Peterborough
8.28 pm	Manchester	Camden	Egginton (GN), Colwick and Peterborough
8.30 pm	Edge Hill	Camden	Egginton (GN), Colwick and Peterborough
8.45 pm	Walsall	Camden	Luffenham, Peterborough, Canonbury (GN)
9.10 pm	Warrington	Camden	Luffenham, Peterborough, Canonbury (GN)

Appendix Three

The Railway Executive's Response to the Inquiry Recommendations

6th July, 1953

MEMORANDUM TO THE RAILWAY EXECUTIVE

ACCIDENT AT HARROW AND WEALDSTONE,
LONDON MIDLAND REGION – 8/10/52

Referring to the Secretary's memoranda of 29th June and 1st July; after examination of the Inspecting Officer's report into the Harrow accident, we are of opinion that the report desired by the B.T.C. should be on the following lines:

With reference to your letter of 30th June, the report of the Chief Inspecting Officer of Railways on the accident which occurred at Harrow and Wealdstone on 8th October, 1952, has been considered by the Railway Executive. They are of the opinion that this report is a very fair one and presents the circumstances in the proper light.

The Executive have no comments to make on the findings and in their opinion the proper conclusion has been reached.

In respect of the Remarks and Recommendations; the Inspecting Officer's remark in paragraph 86 in regard to British Railways standard all-steel coaches and the decision to standardise on buck-eye coupling for main line stock are interesting and bear out the advisability of the decisions which have been made in these respects.

The point made in paragraph 90 in respect of the marshalling of buck-eye vehicles is appreciated and this will be done whenever practicable. It does, however, remain a fact that for some time it will be necessary to mix buck-eye fitted vehicles with screw-coupled coaches.

The only further point calling for comment is in respect of Automatic Train Control, upon which Colonel Wilson gives a very fair exposition of the position to date. The Commission have, of course, been kept informed of the whole of the circumstances and are aware that the tests with the prototype instrument are now well under way between New Barnet and Huntingdon. The Inspecting Officer comments in paragraph 108 on the trial period of six months and it will be noticed that in his opinion this period may have to be longer and thereafter further trials may be necessary with the production design.

Naturally the Railway Executive will wish to limit this period as much as possible but it is, of course, necessary to assess and guard against the failures which arise as a result of the trials. All this work is well in hand and the Executive remain confident that a satisfactory article will be produced within a reasonably short time.

In paragraph 113 reference is made to the other items of signalling equipment necessary for safety purposes. The Executive feel that when the Automatic Train Control programme is authorised it will be necessary to concentrate on this with a view to the expeditious completion of the work but at the same time they will endeavour to provide the other items of signalling modernisation to the limit of their capacity in connection with renewals and new works.

(Sgd.) M. Barrington-Ward	(Sgd.) R.C. Bond	(Sgd) J.C.L. Train
M. BARRINGTON-WARD	for R.A. RIDDLES	J.C.L. TRAIN

Appendix Four

A Letter from Signalman Armitage

A copy of a letter from district relief signalman AG Armitage, the signalman on duty at Harrow No 1 at the time of the accident, probably addressed to the Chief Regional Officer.

33, Strangeways,
Watford,
Herts.

18th October, 1952.

Dear Sirs,

May I please be permitted to express to yourself and all the Senior Officers of the Railway Executive my sincere appreciation of the magnificent way in which I was treated both on the morning of the 8th October at Harrow, and on each occasion since.

I would like to specially thank such officers as Mr Cox, Mr Hearn, Mr Williams, Mr Abrahams, also Mr Rollinson of Harrow Station.

Perhaps you would favour me by your kindness in conveying my appreciation to those officers concerned at some time to suit your convenience.

May I complete this letter, Sir, by once again saying thank you, and closing with a phrase quoted by a fellow signalman which I think aptly describes you all, 'You are dealing with Gentlemen'.

I am, Sir,
  Your obedient servant
    A.G. Armitage
    D.R.S. Watford

Acknowledgements

The author is indebted to those who have so readily responded to his pleas for information and illustrative material for his use in drafting the manuscript to this book. He has received generous help from fellow members of the LMS Society, including: Noel Coates; Gordon Coltas; John Edgington; Niall Ferguson; Keith Miles; John Miller; and Martin Welsh. Likewise assistance has been kindly provided by Leslie Bevis-Smith; Richard Casserley; Andrew Dow; David Hanson; David Hyde; and Don Rowland of the Historical Model Railway Society. Willing support has also come from: Revd John Adis; Bob Berry; Chris Capewell; Clive Carter; Eileen Coey; Jim Connor; Alan Earnshaw; Geoff Goslin; Anthony Gregory; Bernard Harding; Ken Hines; Robert McGowan; John Moss; Margaret Nash; Henry Pryer; Kate Robinson; Peter Rowledge; Derek Smith; Revd John Spinks; and Jimmy Wild; along with those named who have kindly provided their personal recollections and photographs, together with: London Metropolitan Archives; *London Police Pensioner*; Metropolitan Police Museum; National Railway Museum; BR Records Office; *RMT News*; and Transport for London, Archives & Records Management Service. My thanks to them all.

In this edition I am grateful to Mike Blakemore, editor of *Backtrack* for permission to include an article first published in his journal, together with further material from Michael Cobb, Revd Dick Lewis, Malcolm Peakman and Railway Archive (www.railwaysarchive.co.uk).

Bibliography

De Blank, J., Text of the address at memorial service at St Marylebone Parish Church, London, 23rd October, 1952.

Coombs, L.F.E., *The Harrow and Wealdstone Disaster 1952, Twenty Five Years On*, David & Charles, 1977.

Currey, J.H., *Automatic Train Control*, Proceedings of the Institution of Railway Signal Engineers, 1957, p. 388 and 1958, p. 142.

Hall, S., 'Horror at Harrow: caused by chaos in the cab?', *Steam Railway*, September 2002, pp 40-45.

LMS Centenary of Opening of First Main Line, supplement to *Railway Gazette*, 16th September, 1938.

MOT Report, *Double Collision at Harrow & Wealdstone*, HMSO, 1953.

Metropolitan Police, *Report on the Railway Disaster on 8th October, 1952 at Harrow and Wealdstone Railway Station*, 'A' Branch, New Scotland Yard.

Railway disaster at Harrow and Wealdstone station, 8th October, 1952. Report by the Chief Officer, County of Middlesex Fire and Ambulance Service, 16th October, 1952.

Rescue – The Golden Hour, Mentorn Barraclough Carey Productions Ltd, screened on Channel 4 in April 1996.

Rutherford, M., 'Crisis? What Crisis? Coal, Oil and Austerity', *Railway Reflections* No. 71, *Backtrack* No. 11, Vol. 14, (November 2000).

Railway Observer, RCTS, 1952, pp. 301-302, 328 and 1953 p. 219.

Stephenson Locomotive Society Journal, SLS, 1952, p. 307, 1953, pp. 27, 175-176.

Trains Illustrated, December 1952, p. 454.

National and local newspapers.

Index

Abraham, F., RMO, 31, 63
Accidents,
  Bourne End, 111
  Castlecary, 110
  Dagenham East, 113
  Goswick, 111
  Ladbroke Grove, 113
  Quintinshill, 7
  St John's, Lewisham, 6, 113
  Southall, 113
  Welwyn Garden City, 113
Aerial photographs, 20, 32
Air pollution, 4, 7
Air raid precautions, 17
Allen, Dr, 35
Ambulance work, 35, 39, 46, 60, 115
American Air Force contribution, 35
Anderson, Capt., 53
Armitage, A., signalman, 23, 30, 107, 125
Arnold, A.E., newsagent, 26, 57
Armed forces, 17, 50
Assistance by others, 51
Austin, A., Miss, 58
Automatic warning system, 110
Barrington, G., Father, 89
Bennett, C.R., 84
Bonham, D.G., Sdn Ldr, 35
Boots, chemist, 53
Boy & Rover Scouts, 53
Brannan, P., newspaper reporter, 61
Bray, I., Ch. Insp. Police, 47, 59
Breakdown (railway),
  Cranes, 65, 97, 116
  Trains, 65, 116
British Oxygen Co. Ltd, 53
British Red Cross, 53, 115
Brown, R.C., driver, 105
Buck-eye couplings, 27, 124
Camps, K., pathologist, 103
Candey, Jim, Ltd, 47
Carne, radio shop, 53
Cartwright, Sgt, 50
Casserley, H.C., 58
Casualty enquiry offices, 50, 59
Civil Defence, 17, 53
Clarke Co., 54
Clearing the wreckage, 59, 93
Cleaver, J., ASLEF, 103
Cobb, M., Major RE, 60
Cogswell, A.P.L., coroner, 103
Coler, E., Col USAF, 37
Collision, 21
Collyer, A., 56
Composition of trains, 120

Cowper, G., fireman, 123
Cox & Danks Ltd, 53
Cox, L.W., Dist Supt LMR, 65, 84, 116
Darton, W.H., driver, 23
Das, K., Dr, 35
Dean, D., 55
Dennis, solicitor, Middlesex Fire Service, 114
Dickinson, R., PC 574X, 59
Disruption to trains, 83
Diversions,
  Railway, 83
  Road, 49
Double collision, 20
Dow, G., PR&PO, LMR, 30
Dowler, G., fireman, 23
Ely, T., Ambulance Supt, 39
Emergency casualty clearing post, 39
Fagan, M., 49
Fire, 41
Fire Service, 34, 39
Footbridge, station, 11, 26, 29 *et seq.*, 77, 93
Forsyth, I.C., Works Mang. Crewe, 102
Foxley, J., 57
Gaskell, P., Sgt 113X, 34
Graves, Pierce, Dr LMR, 116
Gregory, A.V., photographer, 61
Griggs, W., Sen. Capt & Mrs, S.A., 53
Hall, R.W., traffic apprentice, 31
Halliburton, F.B., driver, 22
Hallmark, J., shift foreman, 23
Hampton, J., driver, 22
Hampton, L., pathologist, 103
Harrison, Dr, 35
Harrow,
  Central Residents Ass., 54
  London Borough, 117
  Rotary Club, 54
  Round Table, 54
  Urban District Council, 53, 54, 91
Harrow & Wealdstone station, 9
Harrow signalling, 11, 13, 105
Hearn, S.G., Oper. Supt LMR, 37, 63
Hepworth, H.E., Branch. Sec. YMCA, 53
Herbert, C.W., 58
Hine, A.R., fireman, 22
Hoare, A., Man. H.W. Perry, 50
Holloway, U.R.S., 103
Hospitals, 41, 56
Illesley, D., Ch. Supr Police, 48
Ivall, D.D., Dep. Ch. Off. Middlesex Fire Service, 116
Jones, S.P., BRB Legal Services, 103
Jones, R.S., driver, 21, 103, 107

Jouning, Major, 50
Kent, J., guard, 31
Kirk & Kirk, Harrow, 53
Kodak Ltd, 53
Krafft, D., PC 158X, 59
Lane, G.T., fireman, 105
Lawrence, A., 84
Lemming, K., PC 487X, 59
Lennox-Boyd, A.T., Minister of Transport, 54
Lindsey, J.S., Dr, 35
Lister, J., Dr, 115
Locomotives, 15
London County Council, 47
London Emergency Services Liaison Panel, 116
London Transport, 33, 65, 83, 84, 88
Loughlin, A.O., councillor, 54
Mail, 49, 81, 84
McAlonan, D., Maj. SA, 53
McIlmoyle, New Works Engr, 58
Medical assistance, 35
Meeking, R., 58
Memorial plaque, 117 et seq.
Merritt, W., guard, 31
Ministry of Transport investigation, 103
Morgan, PC 39X, 34
Mortuary, 35, 39, 47, 59
Moss, J., Dep. Supt Ambulance Off., 60
Mount, A., Lt Col, 111
Nash, W.K., 55
National Emergency Plan, 116
Nixon, Mrs, WVS, 54
Odle, J.E., councillor, 54
O'Sullivan, F., Dr, 35
Parkinson J., fireman, 22
Payne, A.H., p. way ganger, 59
Payne, A.W., driver, 22
Perkins, A., driver, 23
Perry, W.H., Ltd, 50
Personal property, 48, 49, 60, 81
Police activities, 47
Post-war scene, 17
Powis, PC, 49
Press activities, 33
Psychological aspects, 89
Radios, 17, 39, 59
Railway Inspector's investigation, 103
Railway Police, 48, 114
Reaction of staff, 30
Removal of casualties, 39, 55
Renwick, T.D., driver, 35
Rescue operations, 34, 39, 55, 59
Richards, H.J., lengthman, 108

Richards, R., Ch. Off. BTC Police, 115
Richardson, Ch. Insp. Police, 49
Riddles, R.A., Rly Ex. Bd member, 102
Road diversion, 49
Rodgers Coals, 53
Rolinson, C.S., station master, 31, 34
Rolling stock, 15, 117, 120
Rowland, K., PC 362X, 59
Rowlands, L., 34
Rowledge, P., apprentice Crewe, 101
Royal Air Force, 35
Royal Arsenal Co-op. Soc., 47
Ruddock & Meighan Ltd, 53
St John's Ambulance Brigade, 53, 115
Salter, Insp., 50
Salvation Army, 53
Savage, P., Revd., 89
Sayce, C.E., house furnisher, 54
Shaw, F., foreman Crewe, 102
Slade, Insp., 88
Smith, stationers, 39
Spiritual aspects, 89
Stanmore branch, 9, 54, 69, 88
Starmer, T., guard, 105
Steel coaches, 15, 29, 117, 120
Stewart, H.C., Maj. Salvation Army, 116
Stewart, H.E., Revd, 60
Swain, A., apprentice Bow, 58
Sweetwine, A., Lt USAF, 37
Teare, Dr, 103, 107
Telephones, 17, 50, 54, 65
Tersons Ltd, 89
Thorpe, C., lineman, 31
Traffic disruption, 83
Train diversions, 83
Train protection & warning system, 110
Tudor Edwards, R., Dr, 35, 37
Turnock, C., fireman, 22, 103
USAF, 35, 115
Walker, M., PC, 59
Water main, 81
Watkins, J.W., Ch. Reg. Off. LMR, 46, 114
Weiderman, G.P., Lt Col USAF, 37
West, D., Mrs, 60
White, J., Asst Ch. Insp., 116
Williams, S., S&T Engr, 28, 63
Wills, L.K., Dr, 53
Wilson, G.R.S., Lt Col, 103
Winters, M.E., Dr, 35
Wolmuth, H., Dr, 35
Women's Voluntary Service, 39, 53
Wooder, A, Ch. Off. Fire Service, 41, 114
WRAC, 35